Tea

Tea

Viola von Wachendorf

p

Contents

An artistic flower arrangement made of tea leaves known in China as a "green peony" or "tea rose."

Some of the most sought-after varieties of tea in the world grow in the shadow of Mount Everest and the other giants of the Himalayas.

Foreword

Tea is drunk and enjoyed every day all over the world, and is the second most-consumed liquid (after water). For some it is simply a drink; for others it is a philosophy. Many see it as a refreshing thirst-quencher while others associate its preparation with fixed, sometimes elaborate rituals. Whether tea is drunk unadulterated, or with milk or lemon, sweetened or unsweetened, is a matter of taste. The word "tea" derives from the Chinese and occurs today in almost all the world's languages. This is the name by which the drink came to be known in the countries it initially reached by sea (*thé* in French, *Tee* in German, *tè* in Italian). Meanwhile, most of the countries it reached by land adopted a derivative of the more common Chinese pronunciation *cha*. Thus in India, the Arab nations, and the Slavonic world, *chai* is the usual word for tea.

While infusions made from other plants are often also referred to as "tea," strictly speaking the name should be reserved for drinks made from black or green tea proper. The correct term for a fruit or herbal tea is "tisane."

This book offers a brief survey of the wonderful and varied world of tea, for tea is far more than simply a hot (or sometimes cold) infusion. It is a piece of culture and a piece of history—a long, eventful, and occasionally turbulent history. Wars have been waged over tea. The fates of countless individuals and even the world itself have been decided, kings and emperors toppled, peace treaties signed and declarations of war made over cups of tea. But most importantly tea is two things: exquisite pleasure and natural remedy. It has been cultivated in China for around 2,500 years, which means it is probably mankind's oldest cultivated plant.

Join us on a journey to the origins of tea and follow its triumphal march through the centuries and around the world.

Discover a host of valuable and interesting facts about cultivation methods and harvesting, processing, and grading. Let us take you on a tour of the famous growing regions of Asia, Africa, and South America. Learn all about the different varieties, grades, and blends of tea. Pick up some practical hints and tips on how to prepare your favorite tea. Lose yourself for a few pages in the wonderful and exotic world of tea ceremonies, tea rituals, and tea houses. Relax, make yourself a delicious cup of tea and settle down to enjoy a good read, bearing in mind the wise words of the mythical Chinese emperor and scholar Shen Nung:

*"Tea arouses the intellect
and stimulates wise thoughts.
It refreshes the body
and calms the soul.
When you are despondent
it raises the spirits."*

A traditional tea plantation in Asia.
Small paths for the pickers wind between
the serried rows of bright green tea bushes.

The History of Tea

Thought to be the oldest cultivated plant in the world, tea has its origins in China, where it is known to have been grown for around 2,500 years. Even today, guests are greeted with a bowl of tea as a symbol of friendship. In China, tea is served with every meal, serving as a refreshment beforehand and as an aid to digestion afterwards.

While it is claimed that the Chinese knew about tea as long as 5,000 years ago, the oldest reliable records mention dates from 221 BC, when scrolls record the introduction of a tea tax. After AD 879, taxes on salt and tea were China's main source of income.

How tea was discovered

There are countless stories about how tea was discovered. According to one, Emperor Shen Nung (2737–2697 BC), who only drank water after it had been boiled, was the first to drink tea. One day the wind blew three leaves from a tea bush into his bowl and turned its contents brown. The emperor tasted the liquid and found it invigorating and refreshing. From that moment on, so the legend goes, he partook of the delicious drink every day.

Shen Nung was one of the three Yellow Emperors. The Yellow Emperors were gods who lived at first as human beings and gave mankind the gift of knowledge. The "Divine Husbandman," as Shen Nung is known in China, taught the country about the crops millet, wheat, sorghum, soy, and rice, and is regarded as the father of Chinese herbal medicine.

Tea! The unprepossessing dried leaves only surrender their wonderful secrets when brewed with hot water.

The rich green tea bushes hug the gentle slopes of the plantation like a cloak.

Fu Shi, the first of the Yellow Emperors, gave the country the concept of yin and yang, and Huang Ti, the second, gave it acupuncture.

Another legend is of Japanese origin and credits the discovery of tea to Bodhidharma (AD 495). Bodhidharma, the third son of an Indian king, was the first Buddhist missionary in China. While meditating one day, tiredness weighed down on his eyes and he drifted asleep. When he awoke he was so angry at his weakness that he cut off his eyelids and cast them to the ground. There they put down roots and a green-leafed bush sprouted from each one. The Buddhist master tasted the leaves, his tiredness disappeared and he felt wonderfully restored. In Japan the character "cha" is used for both "tea" and "eyelid."

In India there is a story that tea was discovered by the missionary Dharma, who vowed to meditate rather than sleep at night during his seven-year pilgrimage to China. In doing so he hoped to win heavenly support for his missionary work. When, after five years, tiredness overcame him, he got up, and went for a walk among the tea bushes. As he chewed their leaves, his tiredness fell away and he was able to pass the final two years of his pilgrimage without sleeping.

Whether one believes these stories and legends or not, the fact remains that China is considered to be tea's country of origin. It is in this country that the tea plant was first cultivated.

During the Song Dynasty, tea leaves were steamed, ground into a powder, compressed into a wide range of shapes and elaborately decorated.

The development of tea in China

During the Han Dynasty (206 BC to AD 220) tea served as medicine, foodstuff, and sacrificial offering. The Chinese regarded green tea as an effective remedy for tiredness, headaches, lack of concentration, poor vision, rheumatism, and diseases of the bladder.

The first tea master

Under the Tang Dynasty (618–907), the curative drink's stimulating properties were prized especially highly by monks, men of letters, poets, and painters, who composed songs, poems, and stories about tea that have survived to the present day. This was the age of the great tea master Lu Yu, an orphan brought up in a Buddhist monastery, whose great loves were

the theater, writing, and tea. Lu Yu penned a treatise on tea that runs to several volumes. Among other things, *The Classic of Tea*, written in the 8th century, describes 24 different utensils required for making tea. These include items such as bowls from which to drink it and porcelain vessels in which to boil the water.

The author of this hymn of praise to what had by now become a popular drink was honored for many generations as tea's patron saint. His work inaugurated a new way of preparing tea. He recommended that the leaves be harvested in spring, and stressed the importance of the bittersweet quality of tea. Previously, tea had been enjoyed not with milk alone but also with rice and a wide range of additives including cinnamon, ginger, jasmine, and orange peel. Lu Yu himself preferred tea without the addition of milk and spices but placed great emphasis on quality. While many names had been used to describe tea hitherto, it now acquired the standard designation "cha."

The first golden age

Tea culture reached its pinnacle during the Song Dynasty (960–1279). Following an ancient tradition, particularly fine high-quality teas were sent as a tribute to the emperor from every province. Each year the court therefore took delivery of spring tea from the growing regions. The imperial tea was produced in a particular way and given a special name. It had no symbolic significance but was simply of a quality fit for the emperor and his court.

Whereas under the Tang Dynasty tea leaves had still been chopped, ground, and shaped into bricks, during the Song Dynasty they were steamed, pulverized, and then compressed into a wide range of shapes. This resulted in round- and oval-shaped slabs of tea with different surface decorations. Particularly popular were representations of the dragon and the phoenix, the symbols of the imperial couple.

Enthusiasm for tea increased steadily during the Song Dynasty. Emperor Huizong spent a fortune on good tea and wrote a book on the subject. Twenty scrolls long, his work describes how to use the various tea utensils, discusses his preferred quality of tea and urges his people to take more care in their handling of tea. He also wrote a treatise on what he believed to be the 20 noblest varieties. Additionally, Huizong was a painter and calligrapher who painted pictures and wrote poetry on themes relating to tea.

Tea becomes the national beverage

Drinking tea was no longer the preserve of the court and well-to-do. Tea culture had spread throughout the land. A popular game was the "tea contest," a forerunner of the tea competition that still exists today. A fragment of tea slab was placed between sheets of white paper, hammered into small pieces, chopped up finely with a tea knife, pulverized in a mortar and the powder passed through a fine sieve. The finer the powder, the better its ability to float on water and form "flowers." The tea powder was then transferred to a warmed bowl and stirred into a paste through the addition of water. Now began the process known as "water dotting." Water was added drop by drop at short intervals and the mixture whipped with the tea whisk.

A carefully selected jury would examine the hue and evenness of the froth, which was supposed to be white. They would also measure the length of time the tea powder clung to the sides of the bowl. The longer it adhered, the better the verdict.

During the Yuan Dynasty (1271–1368), China was invaded by the Mongols. Powdered tea disappeared and the natural varieties increased in popularity. Green tea began to be processed

It is impossible to imagine the traditional Japanese tea ceremony without a bamboo tea whisk being used to stir or whip the tea.

by steaming the leaves, a technique that is still common today.

New production processes

Up to and including the Ming Dynasty, only green tea was produced in China. It was only when tea started to be transported over large distances that growers began to produce black or fermented tea. Under the Ming Dynasty (1368–1644), China experienced a new cultural golden age. New production processes were developed and tea leaves began to be dried in the sun or roasted in a wok.

Developments in ceramic ware

The transformation in the way in which tea was prepared also manifested itself in the type of ceramic ware used. Leaf tea began to be brewed in a lidded cup through the direct addition of hot water.

This new production technique also influenced the utensils used in the preparation of tea. Whereas tea had previously been boiled up in a large jug or pot, it was now brewed in a lidded cup or teapot, the hot water being poured directly on to the tea leaves. It was around this time that the teapot became the most important item in the preparation of tea. The first teapots were made in the Yixing region. The raw materials used in the manufacture of this uniquely high-quality tea ware, which was to become famous all over the world, were the region's special clays, which occur nowhere else in China. The three types of Yixing clay are known as "red soil," "purple soil," and "green soil."

Mixing the different clays together and firing at different temperatures produces a wide range of colors. These handmade teapots are distinctive for their calligraphic or naturalistic decoration and even today the city of Yixing remains a Mecca for tea lovers all over the world. In Yixing itself tea was drunk not from a bowl or glass but from the teapots themselves, which were small and delicate. This meant that just one utensil was required for making and serving tea. The teapots were small in order to prevent the precious aroma from dissipating too quickly, as happened when larger pots were used.

Another development during this time was that the tea ceremony spread from the monastery to society. Houses started to have small tea altars where incense sticks would be lit to purify the air prior to the drinking of tea.

During the Qing Dynasty (1644–1911), tea found its way all over the world as a trading commodity and techniques for the production of black tea were invented, as the following story relates. During the Opium Wars, foreign troops had occupied a tea factory and were using it as a store house. In the main hall lay the freshly harvested leaf tea, completely unheeded. The leaves began to ferment and emanate a strong scent. Eventually the soldiers allowed the tea grower to check his tea. He subsequently tried to offer his "failed" tea for sale and before long it was indeed bought.

Tea conquers Japan

The Chinese enjoyed a tea monopoly until Buddhist monks introduced it into Japan between AD 520 and 800. There are some grounds for believing that the Zen monks smuggled tea leaves out of the country under their robes.

Another tradition has it that Buddhist monks Saicho and Kukai brought the first tea seeds to Japan in 801. At first, tea was used as a medicine as well as a drink. It was also employed in the monasteries as a stimulant for use during meditation.

The precious commodity was initially reserved for the imperial family and upper stratum of Japanese society and only became more widely available during the 12th century.

Tea has a long tradition in Japan. In 1211 the Buddhist monk Eisai described it as a "medicine that prolongs life."

In 1211 Eisai (1141–1215), a Japanese Buddhist monk who had lived in China for a few years, wrote a two-volume book called *Kissa Yojoki* in which he describes tea as: "A drink with wonderful healing properties, a miraculous medicine that prolongs life."

In 1262 a priest named Eison (1201–1290) distributed tea to the poor and the sick of Nara, a charitable offering that is still repeated every year.

During the 14th century drinking tea became a status symbol among the samurai military nobility. Grand tea contests were held in splendid halls adorned with precious paraphernalia. Over the course of several days, thousands of guests would sample a wide range of teas, and prizes were awarded to those who succeeded in recognizing the different sorts.

The most important event in the development of the tea ceremony (*chanoyu*) was the emergence of the "way of tea" (*chado*), a traditional ritual influenced by Zen and Taoism. Its three main founders were Murata Shuko (1422–1503), Takeno Joo (1504–1555) and Sen no Rikyu (1522–1591). The art of preparing and drinking tea now came to be seen as a way of training oneself to attain a higher spiritual-mental plane. The tea ceremony was therefore no mere aesthetic pastime.

Murata Shuko came from Nara and later traveled to Kyoto where in 1474 he entered a Buddhist monastery to study Zen Buddhism. Of prime importance was his meeting with the renowned Zen master Ikkyu (1394–1481). Shuko held a kind of regular artistic salon that brought together intellectuals, artists, writers, poets, painters, and Noh players. His great contribution was to associate tea with Zen and he thus became the first to hang scrolls by important Zen masters in the picture alcove (*tokonama*) in place of the type of pictures that had previously been common. He placed an emphasis on directing one's gaze inwards and on a contemplation of the simple, essential artifacts of daily life. Under Shuko's influence the tea room became smaller and more sparsely decorated. He preferred the beauty of simple materials and objects.

Charcoal ceremony: fresh charcoal is placed in the hearth at the beginning of the tea ceremony.

The route to Europe

In the 16th century, knowledge of the cultivation and beneficial effects of tea reached Europe with returning Christian missionaries and sailors. The tea trade began with the shipping of tea to Amsterdam by Dutch merchants in 1610. This explains the use of the word "orange" in orange pekoe tea (orange being a color associated with the ruling family of the Netherlands). The tea trade soon spread from Holland to Italy, France, Germany, and Portugal—although initially only green tea was imported. Tea was also transported to Russia, where it was called "cha," by caravans of traders along the Silk Road.

Along with tea, precious Chinese porcelain tea ware was imported into the European marketplace. The original teacups had no handles, as is still usual in Japan and China today.

Germany

The first mention of tea in Germany dates from 1650. It is thought to be Dutch doctor Cornelius Bontekoe, alias Dekker, the personal physician of Elector Frederick William of Brandenburg (the Great Elector), who made tea socially acceptable in Germany.

Because of its high cost, tea was initially confined to the nobility and well off, who regarded it as a cure for flatulence, stomach upsets, and gout. Bontekoe, for example, recommended the drinking of up to 100 cups a day. By the end of the 18th century and beginning of the 19th, tea circles, or literary tea salons, had sprung up.

Renowned all over the world and much sought-after by tea lovers: a Chinese porcelain tea service.

Invitations from the writer Johann Wolfgang von Goethe to his so-called *großer Tee* ("big tea") were particularly cherished. Johanna Schopenhauer, the widow of philosopher Arthur Schopenhauer, also held a tea salon. Among her well-known guests were Ludwig Tieck, Christoph Martin Wieland, brothers Friedrich and August Wilhelm Schlegel, and Prince Pückler. In addition to conversation and lectures, music-making and drawing were also popular activities at her teas.

Tea finally became affordable for ordinary people at the beginning of the 20th century, with afternoon tea becoming fashionable in the 1930s.

East Friesland

East Friesland, the German coastal region to the north-east of Holland, is widely considered to be a land of tea drinkers. Soon after the oriental drink had first been imported by their Dutch neighbors, the East Frisians declared tea, which they normally enjoyed with a dash of rum, to be their favorite drink. They started to import it direct in 1753. The popularity of tea in the region can be partly explained by the very poor

Tea is the favorite drink of the East Frisians, whose teatime tradition dates back to around 1753.

quality of the region's water, which had to be boiled before it could be drunk.

King Frederick II of Prussia (Frederick the Great) wanted to prohibit the drinking of tea in East Friesland. In a declaration of 1777 it was announced that the East Frisians slurped "barbaric quantities" of tea, which was harming their health and had to be stopped. "Old Fritz," as he was popularly known, also criticized tea for encouraging men and women to sit around idly for increasingly longer periods each day. But the East Frisians defended themselves, the ban never came into force, and in the end the drinking of tea was officially sanctioned.

In 1906 the Ostfriesische Teegesellschaft or OTG (East Frisian Tea Company) was founded. East Frisian tea culture now has a dedicated museum in the city of Norden which offers an insight into the different areas of East Frisian life in which tea played a role.

England

Tea was brought to England, where it eventually became the national drink, by the Dutch.

Tea culture was fostered at court primarily by Catherine of Braganza, the consort of Charles II. The Portuguese princess brought a chest of best China tea with her as part of her dowry and introduced aristocratic society to the pleasures of tea drinking.

In 1669 the English entered the tea trade on their own account and tea began to be imported by the English East India Company, which enjoyed a monopoly until 1833.

Trade with China was subject to strict rules. Foreigners were not allowed to set foot on Chinese soil and trade with overseas merchants was therefore conducted in foreign harbors. The tea imported from China was initially paid for with silver coins but was later exchanged for opium, a trade which eventually led to the Opium Wars (after which Hong Kong was ceded to the British) when the Chinese emperor decided to ban British opium imports. By this time Britain possessed colonies in which tea was being successfully cultivated, and thanks to the smuggling into China of a British botanist the fermentation process by which green tea was transformed into the black tea favored in Europe was finally discovered. During the 18th and 19th centuries large tea plantations were established in the colonies with British capital.

The British continued to enjoy the tradition of afternoon tea even when they were thousands of miles from London's elegant tea rooms. This photograph was taken in India c. 1920.

The opening of the Suez Canal in 1868 dramatically shortened the sea route to India and with journey times of under 100 days, more and more tea arrived in Mincing Lane, where the London Tea Exchange and tea importers' warehouses can still be found today. Tea had become a part of everyday life and a commodity well worth taxing.

France

Tea was initially sold in France as a medicine but was considered ineffective by the country's medical profession.

In contrast to the café, where customers often stand at the counter to down a quick coffee, the *salon de thé*, whether on an elegant Paris street or in a provincial marketplace, has these days become a place to relax and linger.

Russia

In the middle of the 17th century, 200 packets of tea were sent to Tsar Michael I as a birthday present. The caravan had traveled from Peking through the Gobi Desert and Siberia all the way to the Volga. This initiated a lively tea trade between China and Russia, and numerous camel trains plied between the Orient and Moscow during the summer months. This "caravan tea" was reputed to be of superior quality to the tea transported by sea, which was stowed in damp, tarred, rank-smelling holds.

When a new railway line opened in Russia in 1880, camel trains fell into decline as a means of transporting tea.

French poster from the 19th century advertising tea and chocolate.

The fresher and more aromatic the tea when it arrived in Britain, the higher the price it could command at auction. The first tea auction was held in London's Mincing Lane. A competition developed among the clipper captains to complete the journey from the Pacific Ocean to the coast of England in the fastest time and tea races were organized by London's tea merchants each season, which have become the stuff of legend. The captain of the first clipper to arrive back with a fresh cargo of tea was rewarded with a handsome cash prize.

In the New World

Dutch merchants shipped tea to New Amsterdam (current-day New York) in around 1650. Water carts were trundled through the streets in an attempt to encourage the town's inhabitants to acquire a taste for the new beverage. At that time only green tea, enriched with numerous exotic spices, was drunk. Before long the new drink had become so popular that tea parties were being held.

Tea also played a role in the beginnings of the American War of Independence. Parliament's imposition of a tax on all goods delivered to the American colonies sparked a boycott of British wares. On December 16, 1773, members of a Masonic Lodge disguised as Mohawk Indians stormed three ships that were lying at anchor in Boston harbor and threw more than 300 chests of imported tea overboard in protest against the tea tax. This historic event, which became known as the "Boston Tea Party," helped to propel America towards independence.

In 1844 America concluded a trade agreement with China, which ended its reliance on Great Britain for tea.

Contemporary illustration of the famous Boston Tea Party. On December 16, 1773, disguised freemasons seized three British ships and threw their entire cargo of tea overboard.

Cultivation and Harvesting

Tea plantations are often planted in terraces on steep slopes. Work on a plantation is exhausting and not without its dangers.

The quality and flavor of tea are determined by the effects of different growing and processing conditions. Region, elevation, and climate in turn influence the character of the individual varieties. The ideal conditions in which to grow tea are mild temperatures of between 64 and 82°F (18 and 28°C) and plenty of sunshine. While superior-quality tea continues to be harvested by hand, machinery is largely being used increasingly on tea plantations. Different growing regions have different harvest times depending on their position.

The tea plant

The tea plant belongs to the camellia family. Two subspecies were originally cultivated. *Camellia sinensis* is a small-leafed bush-like upland plant resistant to cold. Untrimmed, it can grow to a height of 10–13 feet (3–4 meters). *Camellia assamica*, which was discovered in Assam in 1830, is a tropical tree-like plant requiring plenty of warmth.
Left to its own devices, *Camellia assamica* can grow into a magnificent tree 49–66 feet (15–20 meters) tall. Many hybrids have since been

developed throughout the world from these two original species. Tea is an evergreen. Its leaves are shiny and covered in fine hairs when young. The flowers are white or pink and are not used in the making of the drink, even in the case of so-called blossom tea. Neither, generally, is the fruit, although this contains oil which has certain uses. Tea is cultivated in tropical and subtropical regions at heights of 1,970–9,185 feet (600–2,800 meters).

Propagation and tending

The tea plant can be propagated in a number of different ways. While originally grown from seeds or propagated using the layering technique, the method preferred today is the planting of cuttings taken from specially selected parent plants. The young bushes are pruned after the first year in order to encourage them to grow outwards and then trimmed back regularly for a period of three years, by which time they will have attained their final shape and can be harvested for the first time. The broad bushes with outspread branches make the pickers' job easier as the upper leaves are exactly at hand height.

Tea in all its splendor. The luxuriant evergreen with its dense foliage.

Camellia sinensis, *the tea plant, is a small-leafed upland shrub resistant to cold.*

The tea harvest

Harvesting is often carried out by hand—even today. At one time, when drinking tea was the preserve of an elite few, tea leaves were sourced predominantly from wild tea bushes. In China, attempts were made to train apes to pick tea because it was difficult to reach the new shoots on mountainous slopes using ladders.

Even these days, growers in mountainous areas often travel by boat to pick the leaves of wild tea trees growing on islands in mountain lakes. Tea of this kind is particularly valuable, as only

It is still common today for tea to be painstakingly picked by hand, usually by women. Pickers can normally gather 65–75 pounds (30–35 kilograms) per day.

90–175 pounds (40–80 kilograms) of it are produced per year.

In the traditional growing regions, leaves are picked at many different stages during the season, usually by hand. This painstaking method facilitates the traditional differentiation in quality between older leaves, younger leaves, and shoots, which can in turn be subdivided into many different grades. Experienced pickers can be expected to gather 65–75 pounds (30–35 kilograms) per day.

For many premium teas, four leaves are harvested instead of the usual three (a bud and two leaves). Special care is taken to ensure that the leaf stalk is not damaged during picking. The fourth leaf is only removed during the manufacturing process, having helped the shoot and two leaves to remain fresh until as late as possible.

Improving conditions

Not only in the past but also today, those who work in the tea plantations gain little from their hard labor. Agreements now exist between organizations in the countries of consumption and countries of production to improve the living conditions of the pickers and factory workers. Among other things, education and health programs are being supported and home-building projects promoted.

In Darjeeling there are more than 100 tea gardens. Each one is organized like a small village. The employees live with their families on the estates, in which homes and free services such as hospitals, kindergartens, and schools are provided.

Harvesting times

Indian teas, particularly those from the Darjeeling region, are only harvested four times a year.

First flush: tea harvested between March and mid-April.
In-between: somewhat aromatic tea harvested between April and mid-May.
Second flush: the tea picked during the summer between May and June possesses a powerful spicy aroma.
Autumnal: the tea harvested in October and November may not be of the highest quality but has a soft, full-bodied character.

In other regions, such as Sri Lanka (Ceylon) and Sumatra, the climate is conducive to year-round harvesting.

Pickers harvesting the world-famous
Darjeeling tea. This, India's most celebrated
tea, is grown on the southern slopes of
the Himalayas.

Processing and Sorting

The production of green tea

Premium green teas are carefully picked and processed by hand. The traditional Chinese method of tea production involves, first, withering the picked leaves in iron pans on the fire. This kills off the enzymes contained in the leaf cells and prevents any possibility of fermentation. Next, the leaves are placed in small heaps to dry during which stage they are continually separated, turned, and hand-shaped. Gradually the leaves take on their final dark green color. They are then sieved in order to sort the leaves into different sizes.

The latest, most mechanized methods for the manufacture of green tea involve two alternative ways of heating the picked leaves in order to prevent fermentation.

Steaming and roasting

Steaming is the method most commonly used in Japan and the Zhejiang and Anhui provinces of southern China. In order to prevent fermentation, the freshly plucked leaves are briefly steam-treated or plunged into a bath of boiling water.

Sometimes the leaves are "pan roasted" on enormous metal trays in order to achieve the same result. After heating, the leaves are laid out on large trays and rolled. They are then roasted in a large mixing drum containing a

Green tea is finding more and more fans among tea drinkers. The leaves are briefly heated to stop them fermenting.

Even after fermentation there is much work to be done by hand. Here workers are checking and sorting the tea.

number of heating rods. Through the constant turning action and a flow of hot air at a temperature of around 194°F (90°C), water is drawn out of the plant cells and the leaves lose most of their weight. This rolling and roasting process is repeated a set number of times according to the variety. The leaves are then sorted. Sifting machines are used for the simpler varieties while the higher-quality teas are sorted by hand.

The production of black tea

The traditional (orthodox) method for the production of black tea involves four stages: withering, rolling, fermenting, and drying.

Withering: the freshly picked leaves are spread out on meshes and subjected to currents of warm air to speed up the withering process. The leaves lose around 30 percent of their moisture and end up suitably pliable for the next stage.

Rolling: after withering, the (still green) leaves are rolled. For this, machines with two metal plates that slide against each other are used. The leaves are evenly torn, crushed, and cut to enable their sap to react with the oxygen in the air.

Fermenting: the rolled leaves are now spread out on tables and kept damp. This process lasts for two to three hours. The oxygen in the air reacts with the leaf sap and the leaves gradually turn from green to copper red or dark brown. The cells, sap, and scents are broken down further.

Drying: after fermenting the tea leaves are dried in hot air (185°F or 85°C) for around 20 minutes.

The leaves are then sorted using mechanical vibrating sieves, a process that separates out the different sizes of leaf, broken leaf, and leaf fragment. Top-quality teas are subjected to a further hand-sorting in which fragments of stalk and stem are removed.

This traditional or orthodox method is still the only method used for the manufacture of black "Leaf" grade tea.

The CTC method

CTC stands for "crushing, tearing, and curling." During CTC production the leaves are first withered, as in the traditional process, then rolled once before being fed into a machine with serrated rollers that chops them into small pieces. This method tears the cell walls open more quickly and thoroughly than the alternative method. After being run through the machine three or four times the tiny pieces of leaf are then fermented. This processing method produces no "Leaf" and just a few "Broken Leaf" grades but mainly teas of the "Fannings" and "Dust" categories. Most of the tea manufactured using the CTC method is destined for use in tea bags.

The LTP method

LTP is an abbreviation of "Lawrie Tea Processor," a machine named after its inventor, which cuts the tea leaves into very fine pieces with rotating blades. Cold air is blown into the machine at the same time in order to prevent the tea from becoming too warm and the fermentation process being initiated too early. The finely chopped leaf particles then drop directly into the fermentation troughs. This method is suited primarily to the production of "Fannings" and "Dust" grades used in the manufacture of tea bags.

The steaming method was originally developed in Japan. Today gentler steaming techniques are being experimented with in Nepal and elsewhere.

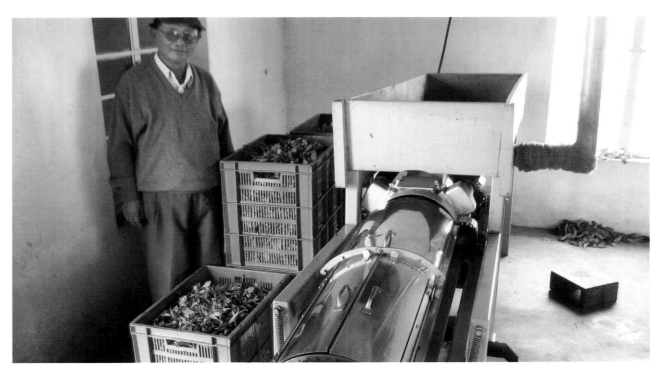

Pickers on the Dambatenne Plantation in Haputale, Sri Lanka, which was founded by Sir Thomas Lipton.

Sorting and leaf grade

Before the tea is auctioned or tasted, it is sorted, either manually or by machine, into different leaf grades. In the case of green and black tea the main categories are Leaf, Broken Leaf, Fannings, and Dust. These categories refer exclusively to the leaf or leaf particle size, not to quality.

Leaf

The term used for tea that consists of whole, practically unbroken, leaves. The aromatic substances are better preserved in whole-leaf teas.

Broken Leaf

Tea made from broken leaves is higher yielding and stronger than Leaf due to the leaves' many breaks and ruptures. It is designated by the letter "B." Teas in this category include: Broken Orange Pekoe (BOP) and Flowery Broken Orange Pekoe (FBOP).

Fannings

This term refers to the small pieces of leaf separated out during the sieving of machine-cut leaves. Orange Fannings (OF) result mainly from the CTC process.

Dust

Dust (D) and Pekoe Dust (PD) are the names used for the results of the final, smallest sieving. The tiny leaf particles are high yielding and generally find their way into tea bags.

Black tea grades

Orange Pekoe (OP)

This tea is made of thin, curled leaves such as the ends of the fine uppermost portions of young shoots.

Flowery Orange Pekoe (FOP)

High-quality tea made from the topmost leaves before they are fully developed. It makes a bright-colored, aromatic infusion.

The first harvest of the year (first flush) is prized by tea lovers for its mild, flowery flavor.

Golden Flowery Orange Pekoe (GFOP)

This is the designation for a Darjeeling Leaf tea consisting of tips and young leaves.

Tippy Golden Flowery Orange Pekoe (TGFOP)

Exceptional quality of Darjeeling tea consisting of a high proportion of tips.

Finest Tippy Golden Flowery Orange Pekoe (FTGFOP)

This is one of the best and most expensive qualities of leaf tea, consisting of a high proportion of tips and buds.

Explanation of terms

Flowery (F): refers to teas from made from very young leaves.

Fluff: the term used to refer to the yellow tea dust that is vacuumed up during production.

Golden (G): describes a tea made partly from golden tips.

Orange (O): regal, noble.

Pekoe (P): from the Chinese word meaning "white down."

Tip: new leaf containing a high proportion of tannic acid that oxidizes lighter or has a silver shimmer due to the white down that covers it.

Tippy: refers to teas consisting of a high proportion of young leaf buds (tips).

Packing and marking

Previously, tea was packed into tea chests after being graded. Today these wooden, foil-lined crates are generally only used for large-leaf tea. Small-leaf types are normally transported in robust paper sacks.

Tea chests were once covered with paper and were often painted with artistic illustrations advertising the firm to which they belonged. Today the essential information is stenciled on their sides. This includes country of origin, leaf grade, gross, and net weight, and picking details (including time).

Tea chests are marked with the country of origin, leaf grade, weight, and picking information (including time).

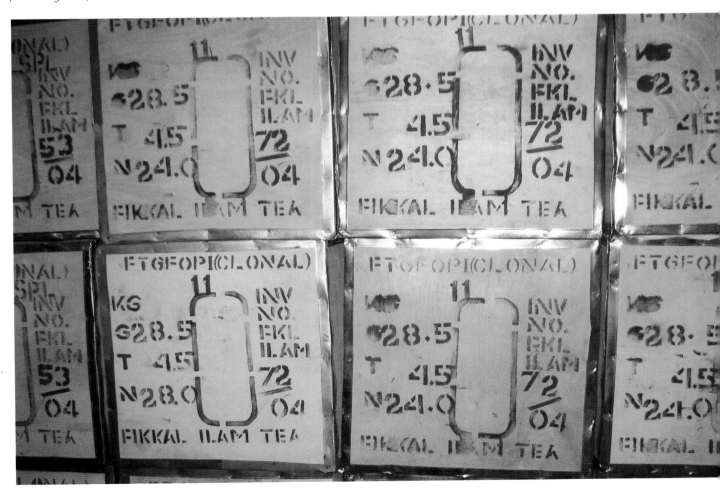

Tea auctions

China is the only place in which tea is distributed via state outlets at fixed prices. In all the other major tea-growing countries it is sold at auction. Tea exchanges are located in, for example, Mumbai (formerly known as Bombay) for northern India, Kochi (formerly known as Cochin) for southern India and Colombo for Sri Lanka. Europe's most famous trading centers are in London and Amsterdam. Tea brokers send importers samples of the tea that is coming up for auction so they can be tasted in advance. Based on the accompanying lists, which provide descriptions of the tea and give the opening prices, international customers can then tell the brokers which teas they are interested in and notify them of the maximum amount they are willing to pay.

A tasting room. Tea tasters taste the dry and infused tea leaves and judge them on the basis of their appearance, color, scent, and taste.

Tasting and testing tea

Before tea reaches the consumer it will have been tested and tasted countless times by the producer, auction house and importer.

Tea tasters check the quality of the tea that is to be auctioned. Only after exhaustive tasting of the tea in question alongside other samples will it be judged and possibly bought. Professional tea tasters also evaluate the ranges of individual suppliers and compose blends.

The criteria

The essential criteria in tasting tea are the appearance, color, scent, and flavor of both the dry and infused leaves. Just as important as the character and taste of the tea are the color of the infusion and the scent emanating from the tasting bowl.

Tasters also assess the initial impression created by the tea in the mouth, the way in which the aroma unfolds, the bouquet, and the aftertaste. From the taste of the tea alone, professional tea tasters can tell everything there is to know about the height at which a tea was grown, the time of picking, and the weather on the day it was picked. This requires experience and patience. In order to be able to assess the tea, tasters need to know all about the different types and their individual nuances of taste. It is not difficult to understand that to learn all this takes years.

Preparation

Tastings always follow the same routine and obey the same standards: the crockery, quantities, and drawing time never vary. Identical amounts of each sample are weighed out (generally one-tenth of an ounce or 2.68 grams). The tea is placed in a lidded brewing cup and boiling water added. After infusing for five minutes, the tea is poured into the tasting bowl through the serrated edge of the cup. The lid containing the infused leaves is then inverted and left to sit on the brewing cup while the spent leaves are subjected to a similar examination as the dry leaf and the liquor itself.

Tasting

The object here is to look, feel, smell, and taste. The dry leaf is thoroughly examined in terms of color, appearance, smell, and cleanliness. The next step is to assess the aroma of the infused leaf.

Finally the liquor is sipped, tasted, and spat out. The tea is sampled either with a spoon or more usually from the bowl itself.

Being a tea taster requires detailed knowledge and years of experience. A professional taster can tell the elevation at which the tea was grown, the time of picking, and what the weather was like on harvest day just from the taste of the tea.

As at a wine tasting, the tester rinses the tea around his or her mouth, then spits it out.

In this brief moment the taster is able to assess all the relevant aspects of the sample. The tea is then described using terms such as "flowery," "fruity," "malty," "spicy," and so on. While there is no standard set of terminology, and sometimes the terms used can contradict each other, below are some of the more common terms in regular use.

Looking, feeling, smelling, tasting, spitting out—these are the routine tasks of tea tasters in the testing lab.

Tasting and testing terms

Dry leaf

Attractive
Uniform leaf in terms of shape and color.

Blend
A mixture of teas.

Bold
Coarse, leaf does not match its grade.

Brownish
Brown coloration resulting from excessively high drying temperature.

Choppy
A hacked-up leaf.

Clean
Evenly sorted leaf free of stalks, dust, and other impurities.

Crepy
Crimped leaves.

Even
Leaf/leaf particles of equal size.

Flowery
Used to describe the tender young leaf.

Gritty
Leaves that are excessively hard.

Irregular
Uneven leaf size.

Melange
Another word for blend.

Milled
Leaf that has passed through a cutter or miller.

Well-twisted
Refers to the dry leaf.

Infused leaf

Aroma
The scent of the leaf after infusion.

Bright
Refers to color.

Dark
Refers to the color of tea leaves after infusion.

Even
Regularity of leaf in terms of color and shape.

Green
Hue caused by excessively short withering, rolling, or fermentation processes.

Mixed
Refers to the uneven coloration of the leaf or the variety of teas in a blend.

Liquor

Body
Fullness of strength and aroma.

Bright
Refers to color.

Clean
With no unpleasant aftertaste.

Coarse
Having an unwelcome aftertaste.

Contamination
Having an alien color and taste.

Dry
Dry taste resulting from excessively long drying phase.

Earthy
Fresh, earthy aroma.

Fruity
Unpleasant taste caused by a bacterial infection.

Hard
Pungent, bitter taste.

Malty
A desirable taste reminiscent of malted grains.

Moldy
A stale or musty, undesirable taste.

Scorched
Impaired taste and/or color due to over-firing.

Smoky
Smoky taste caused by a non-airtight drying device.

Spicy
Highly flavored.

Thin, weak
An infusion lacking body.

Flowery, malty, spicy—the verdict of the tea taster is both a description and a seal of quality.

Growing Regions Around the World

Green and black tea is produced in Asia, Africa, South America, Australia, and Europe (the Azores and Turkey).

Asia

Freshly picked tea leaves from a plantation in Kandy, Sri Lanka, one of the world's main tea-growing regions.

China

Tea is cultivated in all the central and southern provinces of its traditional homeland, China. In the south this includes the provinces of Anhui, Fijian, Guangdong, Guangxi Zhuang, Guizhou, Hainan Dao, Henan, Hubei, Hunan, Jiangsu, Jiangxi, Shaanxi, Sichuan, and Yunnan. The best teas are grown at elevations of between 3,280 and 8,200 feet (1,000 and 2,500 meters).

In China's southern provinces there are several hundred tribute gardens, many of which are connected with the Buddhist monastic tradition. The tea produced by these gardens was once reserved for the emperor and his household. Tribute tea could only be picked by white-clad, freshly washed virgins, and collected in silver baskets under the supervision of a trusted imperial servant. Only the bud and sometimes the topmost leaf were allowed to be gathered, and these were in fact snipped from the bush with shears. The strictest attention was paid to ensure that there was no possibility of the tea being sullied as a result of being handled or gazed upon by ordinary mortals.

Most of the tea produced in China is green tea. Chinese black tea, which is distinctive for its soft but aromatic taste, is manufactured for export only.

Taiwan (Formosa)

Tea has been cultivated on Taiwan since 1870. Specialties of the island, which is economically and politically independent of China, are semi-fermented oolong teas whose tastes lie halfway between those of green tea and black tea. Traditionally the first harvest begins on April 20 and reaches its climax on May 6. Black tea is

produced mainly in the Sun Moon Lake region. The main types of green tea produced on the island are Sencha and Gunpowder.

Japan

Japan produces only green tea. The best growing conditions are in the south of the main island Honshu as well as on Shikoku and Kyushu. Black tea is imported for domestic use. Japan's most famous tea is grown in Udi near Tokyo in the province of Shizuoka.

India

Tea has been cultivated in India since the first half of the 19th century. Today India is responsible for around a third of the total world tea harvest.

Assam

Assam, a state in north-east India, is where the tea plant *Thea assamica* was discovered. The plateau on either side of the Brahmaputra River is the largest continuous growing region in the world. The first flush is harvested extremely early, in February, and has a soft,

fresh, flowery flavor and a bright yellow-gold color. The highest-quality Assam teas are harvested between May and the end of June (second flush).

Darjeeling

The cultivation of tea in Darjeeling, a town in northern India, began in 1841 when one Dr. Campbell, stationed there as medical officer and later sanitorium superintendent, planted tea seeds in his garden. Following a period of successful experimentation, the British government decided to establish tea nurseries in the area.

The first tea gardens were Tukvar, Steinthal, and Aloobari. India's most famous tea-growing region is located on the southern slopes of the Himalayas. As on the Assam plateau, the conditions are ideal for growing tea.

The tropical heat, humidity, mountain coolness, and monsoon rains promote fertility and maturity. The leaves are picked exclusively by hand. Darjeeling is also known as the "Queen of Teas." It produces a light infusion with a delicate, flowery taste. Most of the harvest is processed as Leaf-grade tea.

A tea plantation in India, whose history of tea cultivation dates back to the 19th century. Today a third of the world's tea is harvested in India.

The harvested leaves are brought to central mustering points, loaded on to lorries, and taken away to be processed as quickly as possible.

However, Darjeeling is not always what it seems. Throughout the world countless teas are sold under this famous name that actually originate in other regions and the Indian government has now introduced a specific trademark for "Darjeeling Tea" in order to certify its authenticity on every invoice and every packet.

Other Indian producers

Tea is also grown and processed in the Sikkim, Dooars, and Nilgiri areas of India. The tea produced in the state of Sikkim, located to the north of Darjeeling, displays a similar character to that of its neighbor.
Dooars lies between Assam and Darjeeling. The light-brown infusion produced by the locally grown tea is aromatic and mildly spicy, and is used mostly for blending.

In the Nilgiri highlands of southern India, tea is grown in the states of Karnataka, Kerala, and Tamil Nadu. The delicate, soft, lemony aroma of Nilgiri tea, which is grown at elevations of between 2,625 and 6,560 feet (800 and 2,000 meters) is attributed to the dry season around the turn of the year. The tea plantations of this region are mostly managed by small farmers, and the tea is processed using both orthodox and machine methods.
Bangladesh, the second largest nation on the Indian subcontinent, also produces a significant amount of tea.

Sri Lanka

The cultivation of tea on Sri Lanka (formerly Ceylon) started around 100 years ago. Previously the island had been the world's

Harvesting tea in the Nilgiri hills in south-west India.

Nepal

The Himalayan kingdom of Nepal borders Tibet (China) to the north and India to the south and west, and is one of the world's youngest tea-producing nations.

In 1863 Mr. Gajaraj Singh Thapa, brother-in-law of the prime minister and governor of the province of Ilam, founded the Ilam Tea Garden with seeds from China. The first tea factory was built in 1873, although most of the country's plantations are far more recent.

In the mid-1950s the United Nations launched a development project to promote and provide financial support to the professional cultivation of tea in Nepal.

Most Nepalese tea production uses the orthodox method and adheres to the very latest ecological standards. In terms of taste and

second-largest coffee producer but its coffee plants were wiped out by rust fungus. In 1860, James Taylor, a young Scot, planted the island's first tea cuttings and experimented with growing tea, and it was not long before large-scale cultivation occurred. Today Sri Lanka is the third-largest producer of tea in the world.

Although Sri Lanka is now independent, its tea is still marketed under the old colonial name of "Ceylon." The island boasts particularly good growing conditions and, depending on the elevation at which it is grown, its produce is referred to as low-grown (up to 2,135 feet/ 650 meters), medium-grown (2,135–4,265 feet/ 650–1,300 meters), and high-grown (over 4,265 feet/1,300 meters). Tea is now cultivated in two main regions of the island:

Nuwara Eliya, known for short by the Sinhalese as Nurelia, Sri Lanka's highest growing region. Only the finest types grow here during the north-east monsoon.

Dimbula, which lies to the west of the central mountain range. The region's dry climate provides the right conditions for tea of the highest quality.

Pickers at work in Oothu, southern India, one of the world's most famous tea-growing regions.

general character, the tea grown in Nepal resembles that of Darjeeling.

Africa

The cultivation of tea on the African continent began in the early years of the 20th century.

Burundi

Burundi's tea gardens, located at a height of around 6,560 feet (2,000 meters), produce small quantities of exceptionally high-quality tea.

Cameroon

In Cameroon, mostly black CTC tea is grown on the fertile slopes of Mount Cameroon.

Kenya

Kenya's tea plantations are located in the highlands above Lake Victoria. The climate favors year-round harvesting. Kenyan tea is almost exclusively black, manufactured using the CTC method.

Malawi

Malawi's main tea-growing areas can be found in the southern district of Mulanje, where the crop can be harvested year-round. Most of Malawi's production is used for blending.

Mozambique

Broken Leaf tea destined mainly for tea bag blends is grown in tea gardens at around 3,280 feet (1,000 meters) above sea level.

Rwanda

During the political unrest of the 1990s the tea factories were destroyed and the tea bushes ruined—or at best badly neglected. Most of the factories have now been restored and modernized, and the plants have regenerated.

Tanzania

Tea was first planted in Tanzania by German settlers in 1905. Today the country's tea estates are located in central northern and southern regions at elevations of 3,280–6,560 feet (1,000–2,000 meters). Black tea is produced here using the CTC method.

When harvest time arrives it is essential to proceed quickly in order to gather and process the tea at peak condition. Hundreds of workers are deployed across the large estates to pick the leaves in as short a time as possible.

A particularly strong tea grows in Bandung on Java (Indonesia). It is very good for blending.

Zimbabwe

The handful of tea gardens in what was once Rhodesia are located at heights of 3,280–4,595 feet (1,000–1,400 meters) and the bulk of their harvests are processed into tea bags or powdered tea.

South America

Argentina

Tea has been grown in the Chaco, Corrientes, Formosa, Misiones, and Tucumán regions of Argentina since the beginning of the 20th century and is generally used for tea bags or instant tea. The country has also started to produce small amounts of green tea.

Ecuador

The Te Sangay estate, founded in 1962, was Ecuador's first tea plantation. The country's tea factories now produce CTC tea and tea processed into tea bags.

Peru

Peru's first experiments with tea seeds were conducted in 1913 but it was not until 1928 that the country's first tea plantations were successfully established. Today the main growing areas, whose cooperative factories produce black tea, are located in Cusco and Huanuco. Limited quantities of green tea are also produced in other areas.

Other regions

Australia

Tea has been commercially grown in Australia since 1960. The leaves are harvested mechanically and processed into black tea for tea bags. Green tea is produced in small quantities in Madura.

Indonesia

Tea is produced all year round on the Indonesian islands of Sumatra and Java, and also in Malaysia. Its strong taste means it is well suited to blending.

Portugal

The first tea gardens were laid out on São Miguel in the Azores in 1945. They are harvested several times between May and September—many of them still by hand—and the leaves processed into green and black tea.

Turkey

Black tea of a light, pleasant character is produced in Rize in north-eastern Turkey.

The Different Types of Tea

Only the white leaf buds and very young silvery tips are used to make white tea. In China white tea was once reserved for the exclusive use of the emperor and his household.

It is commonly believed even today that green and black tea originate from different plants. The real difference, however, is that black tea is fermented and green tea is not. During the Qing era it was discovered that fermenting and drying the leaves allowed them to be kept for longer. There are many different varieties of tea, each of which belong to one of the following main types.

Green tea

For the better qualities of green tea only the first two leaves and the bud are picked. During harvesting, care must be taken to ensure that the leaves are not damaged as this would set the fermentation process in train. The leaves are briefly heated or steam-treated before being rolled and then dried.

Good quality is indicated by a fresh scent resembling that of hay and by green rather than brown leaves that are dry and firm with a dull sheen.

After infusing it is easy to tell whether the tea has been made from tips or whole leaves. It is also possible to see whether the leaves have been manually picked or cut with a knife and whether the leaves have started to ferment, in which case they will be speckled brown.

Oolong tea: the manufacture of "black snake" tea is one of the most difficult and painstaking of all tea production processes.

White tea

Chinese white teas, which have a particularly delicate flavor, are made from a special "white" variety of tea plant. Only the white leaf buds and very young silvery tips are picked for this exquisite tea. The Chinese name for the white hairs that cover the young leaves is *bai hao*, which was transcribed into English as "pekoe."
In spring, when the buds start to appear, the silvery-white shoots are picked by hand. They are dried in the sun but are not heated, rolled, or crushed. The buds remain complete and provide the tea with its delicate floral aroma.
For a long time white tea was destined for the Chinese emperor alone. It was highly prized for its subtle aroma and was considered a magical, life-prolonging drink. It is still highly valued in China today.

Oolong tea

The meaning of oolong, a type of tea first manufactured during the Ming Dynasty, is "black dragon" or "black snake." According to legend, the owner of a tea garden was so frightened by a black snake that he took flight and only returned to his dried tea leaves after several days. In the intervening period the leaves had oxidized in the sunshine and made a highly aromatic beverage when infused. Oolong is a semi-fermented tea, although there is considerable variation in the degree to which it is actually fermented. It is considered one of the most difficult teas to make.
The picked leaves are spread out on a cloth in the sun for about an hour, during which time a mild fermentation occurs. To assist fermentation, a number of oolong varieties are shaken in bamboo baskets. This tears the edges of the leaves, enabling the sap to emerge.
Depending on the particular variety, the leaves are then moved inside for a further period of

Black tea

In East Asia, black tea is actually known as "red tea." As with green tea, best-quality black tea is made from the top two leaves and a bud. After harvesting, the tea is spread out to dry on a wire-mesh frame for between 12 and 18 hours. During the ensuing fermentation process, leaf and cell sap react with the oxygen in the atmosphere, are transformed, and the "black" tea acquires its reddish hue and characteristic flavor. Fermentation also renders the tea particularly long-lasting.
Once the fermentation process has finished the tea is graded by leaf size.

fermentation or for processing. The withered leaves are loaded into the heating drum and dried for roughly 45 minutes at 158°F (70°C). The hot leaves are then tipped into clean cotton cloths that are tied into large bales and rolled continually for 20 minutes in a kneading and crimping machine. Thereafter the leaves are tipped back into the heating drum and reheated. This procedure can be repeated up to ten or so times, depending on the type of oolong being produced. The oxidation process is interrupted when the edges of the leaf have turned black but the middle is still green. At the end of the production process the leaves are heavily and firmly rolled, then subjected to a final roasting process in order to ensure that the tea will keep well. Four different basic types of oolong are made.

Pouchong

This copper-colored tea is up to 12 percent fermented. The infusion has a fruity scent and a delicate bitter-sweet flavor.

Zhen Cha Oolong

The leaves of this tea are up to 30 percent fermented and more tightly rolled. The infusion has an intensely fruity taste, and is dark and very full-bodied.

Tea sorted by leaf grade, which designates the leaf or leaf particle size of the finished product. The four main categories are: Leaf, Broken Leaf, Fannings, and Dust.

So Cha Oolong

During the production process the leaves are tightly rolled and up to 50 percent fermented. The tea has a sweet, smoky flavor.

Kao Shan Cha Oolong

This upland tea is up to 30 percent fermented. The tea has a green-gold color and a delicate, astringent flavor.

Pu-erh tea

Long known in China, pu-erh tea, which takes its name from a small town in the Chinese province of Yunnan, is currently acquiring more and more of a following in Europe too. This choice tea is used in traditional Chinese medicine to alleviate a wide range of complaints. Green pu-erh, made from the tender spring harvest, is first steamed and then treated with bacterial cultures in a special process involving the addition of microorganisms. The tea is either packed loose or compressed into small concave cakes and stored for months in cool conditions. The tea has a mild taste and is greenish in color.

Red pu-erh is made in a similar way to green pu-erh, but from the large summer harvest. After processing it is pressed into boxes and aged for a long time during which it acquires its red hue and earthy taste.

Tea originated in China. It is still cultivated in all the country's southern provinces, where the best qualities are grown at elevations of 3,280–8,200 feet (1,000–2,500 meters). One of the most important growing regions lies in the province of Yunnan.

Classic Varieties and Blends

Chinese classics

China is the main producer of green tea, which normally has a slightly tart, smoky flavor. The best-known varieties of green tea include the following.

Chun Mee

This tea has a fresh and slightly tart flavor. It is produced not only in China but also in Taiwan, India, and Indonesia.

The leaves of Gunpowder tea are rolled into tight pellets and unfold like tiny flowers when infused.

Gunpowder

Gunpowder tea is made in China and Taiwan. It takes its name from the appearance of the leaves, which are rolled into tight pellets and unfold like tiny flowers when infused. The tea produces a yellow-green infusion with a fresh, tart taste.

Lung Ching (Dragon Well)

This tea is a specialty of the Zhejiang growing region. It is distinctive for its delicate aroma and is one of China's finest varieties.

Pi Lo Chun

This tea, produced in China and Taiwan, has spiral-shaped leaves and a mildly flowery taste.

Well-known black teas

Keemun

This black tea from the Chinese province of Anhui is distinctive for its regularity of leaf and has a smooth, sweet, fruity taste.

Lapsang Souchong

This Chinese tea is made by drying the large leaves over a pine needle or pine resin fire. It is also used in Russian blends.

Flower magic

Particularly fine varieties of tea are often processed into fascinating shapes and constructions. A mass of hand-picked leaf tips are carefully rolled after steaming and sewn into the shape of a flower, which is then left to dry and form a flat rosette.

These artistic flower arrangements are known in China as "green peonies" or "tea roses" after the flowers they resemble. Each one corresponds exactly to the amount of tea required for one large cup and can be infused as many as six times.

These painstakingly assembled green tea flowers attain their full beauty when steeped in hot water. They often conceal buds that open out into three chrysanthemum flowers, for example, which then rise up slowly to the surface. The best way to observe the unfolding of these flowers is by infusing them in a glass cup. Jin Shang Tian Hua (Anhui) and Mu Dan (Yunnan) are good examples of teas of this type.

The number of leaves of a "tea rose" corresponds exactly to the amount of tea required for one large cup.

Lung Ching tea is one of China's finest varieties.

Genmaicha tea is a blend of Sencha tea leaves and roasted wholegrain rice which tastes of popcorn.

These artistic teas, sometimes referred to as display or craft teas, are now available in a wide range of designs and will surprise the observer by forming balls or cones, baskets or pagodas, concealing buds that bloom into roses, carnations, amaranthuses, jasmines, or lilies. They offer a wonderful display of shapes and colors that can turn afternoon tea into a spectacular event. Display teas also make an ideal gift for serious tea lovers.

Japanese classics

After China, Japan is the second-largest producer of green tea, whose flavor is distinctive for its notes of fresh grass.

Sencha

This green tea is Japan's most popular everyday tea. Processing begins immediately after the tea is picked. The leaves are steamed briefly, shaken in a current of hot air and dried until (after rolling) they look like green needles. Different qualities of Sencha are produced depending on the time of year when they are harvested. For average-quality teas the leaves are picked by machine.

Bancha

This green tea contains a lot of tannins and little caffeine. *Ban* means something like "coarse" or "ordinary" and indeed Bancha is made from older and larger leaves. The name "three-year-tea" probably refers to the fact that leaves up to three years old are harvested to make Bancha. This simple tea is enjoyed as an everyday tea in its country of origin.

Gabalong

This specialty tea with a mild and delicate aroma is regarded in Japan as a health drink. Gabalong contains many of the ingredients that are thought to make green tea so healthy.

Genmaicha

This variety is made by blending Japanese Sencha with roasted wholegrain rice, which gives it a popcorn flavor.

Gyokuro

This tea, which is also known as "Precious Dewdrop," is one of the finest and most expensive of Japanese varieties. As soon as the new buds appear the tea plants are covered with reed mats and dark nets. During harvesting, which takes place in May, only the tenderest shoots are picked.

Kukicha is a Japanese specialty tea made partly from stems and stalks.

As the leaves are exposed to very little light, they contain fewer tannins and have a milder flavor than other varieties of green tea.

Kokeicha

This powdered tea is pressed into the shape of pine needles with the help of rice starch.

Kukicha

To make this specialty tea, stems, and stalks are processed along with the leaves. Kukicha has a light, fresh flavor and makes a pale yellow infusion.

Matcha

This is the famous green tea used in Japanese tea ceremonies. It is manufactured by stone-grinding best Sencha leaves into a fine powder.

Shincha

A top-quality green tea. Each new harvest is eagerly awaited in Japan.

India

Assam

Assam tea (e.g. GFBOP, TGBOP, FTGFOP) has a strong, spicy, and aromatic flavor. This black tea often forms the basis for East Frisian blends.

Darjeeling Autumnal (FOP + GFOP)

This black tea grown on the southern slopes of the Himalayas is harvested between October and November after the monsoon. It is distinctive for its light, delicate aroma, and contains low levels of tannic acid.

Darjeeling First Flush (FTGFOP)

This light and subtle black tea from the southern slopes of the Himalayas is harvested in February and March. Some European countries refer to it as "flight tea," as most of it is exported by airplane to Europe each spring.

Matcha, Japan's famous premium-quality green tea, is used in the country's traditional tea ceremony.

Ceylon (Sri Lanka)

Dimbula (OP + FOP)

This black tea is distinctive for its strong spicy flavor and mildly lemony fragrance. It is harvested between December and March.

Nuwara Eliya (GFOP)

This is a black tea with a fresh, sharp flavor and mildly lemony fragrance. It is harvested all year round.

Ceylon Uva (FOP)

Uva possesses a hearty, tangy flavor with a hint of lemon. This high-grown tea, cultivated at 4,265–8,200 feet (1,300–2,500 meters) above sea level, is harvested between July and September.

Scented teas

China is also responsible for classic scented teas such as rose and jasmine tea, whereby green tea or sometimes a blend of green tea and black tea is given a particular fragrance through the addition of flower blossom. During this process the blossom is regularly sieved out and replaced.

China's jasmine blossom tea is a light green tea scented with jasmine. In traditional Chinese medicine this tea is reputed to have a balancing influence on yin and yang and also to promote circulation of the qi life force.

The perfumed teas made in Europe generally result from various essences or essential oils being added after, rather than during, the production process. This involves different aromas being sprayed evenly over the tea

A colorful and tasty blend containing fruit and herbs.

A selection of cookies to accompany afternoon tea.

Breakfast tea

A typical English Breakfast tea consists of two-thirds fruity Ceylon tea and one-third powerful Assam.

Afternoon tea

A blend of Ceylon and Assam teas is ideal to round off lunch or to enjoy in the early afternoon.

Five o'clock blend

This blend consists of Ceylon Orange Pekoe or Flowery Orange Pekoe with a little Darjeeling. It is a strong tea usually enjoyed with milk and sugar, and often accompanied by shortbread cookies, wafers, ginger cookies, thinly cut sandwiches, or buttered toast with jam.

in slowly revolving drums. These scents include fruits, spices, and flavorings such as cherry, maracuya, vanilla, cinnamon, and aniseed. Citrus flavors such as orange, lemon, and bergamot (as in Earl Grey) are also extremely popular.

Classic blends

Most commercial teas are blends. There are two types: blends from different tea gardens within a particular region; and blends, such as East Friesian and English Breakfast, from different growing regions. Large tea merchants have tasting departments staffed by specialists who are responsible for maintaining the consistency of blends in terms of taste, quality, and price.

The exact proportions of the different teas that constitute these blends tend to be a very well-kept secret. Successful blends are generally marketed under the company name.

Ceylon and Assam blends are stronger than Darjeeling blends. They can be drunk with sugar, brown rock candy, milk, or lemon according to taste.

China Caravan

The name of this tea recalls the caravans that once transported China tea to Russia. It is a mild, aromatic blend of green, in other words unfermented, teas.

China White Tips

This is a blend of Tarry Souchong or Lapsang Souchong and non-smoked Chinese varieties. It has a mildly smoky, aromatic flavor.

English blend

This is the name by which blends of Ceylon, Indian, and Chinese tea are known. Leaf grade is not important here.

East Frisian blend

A good East Frisian blend consists of two-thirds Assam and one-third Ceylon or Sumatra/Java.

Iced tea is a refreshing thirst-quencher for the hot summer months.

Earl Grey

Earl Grey is a mixture of Darjeeling, Assam, Ceylon, and Chinese Keemun tea. Both green and black teas are used. It is scented with bergamot oil, which gives it its distinctive citrusy flavor. This blend is named after Charles Grey, the 2nd Earl, William IV's prime minister 1830–1834. He would probably have received it as a diplomatic gift, and some sources say he was given the recipe by a Chinese mandarin.

Instant tea

Instant tea is made by brewing up large quantities of tea in special factories. The resulting liquid is then freeze-dried or dried in hot air, and the tea solids granulated or powdered and packed into jars.

Iced tea (ice tea)

Iced tea is a summer drink particularly popular among Americans. It is made by brewing green or black tea rather more strongly than usual and pouring it over ice cubes while still warm. The tea acquires its particular aroma from this

rapid cooling process, remains clear, and loses any bitterness.

Iced tea first came to attention in St. Louis in the United States in 1904. During the World Fair, merchant Richard Blechynden is supposed to have poured hot tea into a glass over ice cubes and served it in place of the usual iced drinks.

The iced tea widely distributed today is usually a flavored instant tea and has little to do with the original drink. Yet good iced tea is extremely easy to make from scratch.

Fruit and herbal infusions

Real tea is made from the *Camellia sinensis* plant or its subspecies. The correct name for infusions made from other plants are tisanes, although they are also commonly referred to as fruit and herbal teas. The particular parts used—fresh or dried—vary from plant to plant. A wide range of herbs is used in folk medicine for the treatment of minor complaints. Here is a small selection of the most common herbs, fruits, and spices that are used either alone or in blends to make medicinal teas.

Aniseed (Pimpinella anisum)

This sweet infusion is made from the small gray-brown fruits of the aniseed plant. It aids digestion, is good for the circulation and is also used as an ingredient in children's teas.

Apple (Malum)

Apple tea is made from the fruit and peel. It calms the nerves and promotes sleep.

Camomile (Matricaria chamomilla)

Tea made from the fresh or dried flowers of the camomile plant not only tastes good and is wonderfully aromatic but, thanks to its particular active ingredients, it also relieves cramp, and has anti-inflammatory and antibacterial properties. Camomile tea is a popular home remedy for complaints of the stomach and intestines. It can be used externally (as a bath essence, for example), and is also effective against skin problems and inflammations.

Cinnamon (Cinnamomum zcylanicum)

This aromatic sweet tea is especially good served with apple desserts. Cinnamon is a natural remedy for a number of minor ailments.

Dandelion (Taraxacum officinale)

The infusion made from the dried taproots and leaves of the dandelion has a slightly bitter taste. It has blood-cleansing, diuretic, and anti-rheumatic properties, and also stimulates the appetite.

Fennel (Foeniculum vulgare)

The seeds of this plant possess calming and mucus-dissipating properties. The sweet-

Aniseed, fennel, and cinnamon: three spices commonly used to make medicinal teas or added as flavorings to traditional teas.

Hibiscus (Rosemallow)

This infusion is made from the fleshy calyx of the hibiscus and has a sourish fruity taste. The drink has a relaxing effect on both the stomach and the intestine. The plant is also used to spice and color many other fruit and herbal teas.

Honeybush tea (Cyclopedia intermedia)

Honeybush tea, whose other names include *Bergtee* and *Kaptee*, is made in South Africa. Honeybush is a shrub that grows on slopes and in mountainous areas. It gets its name from the fragrance of its flowers. The shoots and flowers are picked, dried, and then fermented in an oven at high temperatures.

The positive effects of the tea, which contains a range of trace elements including potassium, calcium, zinc, manganese, and iron, have

Ginger works its full magic as an aid to digestion when brewed as an infusion. The active ingredients of this exotic tuber are known to relieve stomach and intestinal complaints.

tasting infusion is effective against digestive complaints, flatulence, and colic.

Garlic (Allium sativum)

Garlic is valued in many cultures for more than just its taste. Its antibacterial, antimycotic, and mildly hypotensive properties are also well known, as is its ability to improve blood flow.

Ginger (Zingiber officinale)

Ginger promotes digestive health, helps relieve cramps, stomach, and intestinal complaints, and stimulates the circulation. It also acts as a sudorific (induces sweat) and in this capacity is used in the treatment and prevention (by boosting the body's own immune defences) of colds.

Ginseng (Ginseng radix)

Also known as the "life root," ginseng is one of the oldest known medicinal plants and numerous healing properties are attributed to it. These include improving alertness and powers of reaction, boosting the immune system, and improving general health.

been known for around 200 years to relieve a range of complaints—particularly those of the respiratory organs.

In its native South Africa, Honeybush is often preferred to black tea thanks to its natural honey-like sweetness. As it contains virtually no caffeine, it is an ideal drink for the evening.

Java tea (Orthosiphonis folium)

Java tea is also known as "cat's whiskers" because of its extremely long stamens. It is indigenous to south-east Asia and Australia. The leaves are also sold as a wonder drug under the name "kidney tea."

The plant possesses diuretic and mild antispasmodic properties, and the infusion made from it is therefore used as a remedy for urinary retention and other complaints of the bladder and kidneys.

Lapacho tea (Tabebuia impetiginosa)

Lapacho tea, also known as Inca tea, is obtained from the red-brown inner bark of the South American Lapacho tree. The South American Indians have used the bark as a remedy for all kinds of complaints from time immemorial, passing on from generation to generation knowledge about its healing powers and varied uses.

The bark grows darker in color the closer it gets to the outside of the tree. The bark that grows back again within a year is stripped off, ground, boiled, and an extract obtained. The resulting aromatic tea is rich in tannins and minerals. Lapacho is enjoyed as a tasty beverage but is also used as a secondary treatment for a range of complaints including bronchitis, anaemia, diabetes, and inflammations of the stomach lining, and is drunk as a prevention against

The classic of medicinal teas: camomile tea is made from fresh or dried flowers. It relieves cramp, and has anti-inflammatory and antibacterial properties.

cancer. It is also used externally as a remedy for eczema, abscesses, and fungal infections.

Lemon balm (Melissa officinalis)

The dried leaves of this plant, also known as "melissa," are used to make an aromatic infusion. Lemon balm tea smells wonderfully fresh, is an antispasmodic, and has relaxing and calming properties. It is used above all to counteract sleeplessness and alleviate tension. Thanks to its pleasant taste, lemon balm is used as an additional ingredient in many herbal tea blends.

The "green gold of the Indios." Mate tea originated in Brazil and is available either green or roasted.

Aromatic peppermint tea is a long-standing household remedy against a wide range of complaints.

Lime blossom (Tilia)

There are two types of lime: winter lime (*Tilia cordata*) and summer lime (*Tilia platyphyllos*). The flowers and end-of-twig leaves of both continue to exude a mild honey-like scent even after drying. The infusion is calming and has sudorific properties. It is used above all as a remedy for colds and chills, and to clear the respiratory tracts.

Mate tea (Ilex paraguayensis)

Mate tea originated in Brazil. The "green gold of the Indios," as it was called by the Europeans, is made from the leaves of various species of holly (*Ilex*) and is available either green or roasted. The leaves are withered and dried in order to produce the tea. Various health benefits are attributed to mate. It is thought to alleviate mental and physical fatigue, aid digestion, and stimulate the metabolism.

Peppermint (Menthae piperitae)

The leaves alone or leaves and chopped-up stem of this plant (which originated in England) are used to make a cool and refreshing tea that is effective against stomach and intestinal problems, flatulence, nausea, and headaches. It is also used to enhance the taste of other herbal teas. Peppermint oil is a tried-and-tested remedy for headaches.

Rooibos (Aspalathus linearis)

This South African tea-like plant, whose name means "red bush," is used to make a colorful and delicious-tasting herbal tea. Also known as "Massai tea," it is caffeine-free, low in tannins, and makes an ideal drink for children as well as adults.

Rooibos is mildly calming and soporific. It contains active ingredients that boost the immune system, and are effective against stomach and intestinal problems.

Rose hip (Rosa canina)

This tea is prepared from the fruit of a particular kind of rose plant, the Dog Rose. It has a fruity, slightly sour taste, contains vitamin C, and helps combat colds by boosting the body's powers of resistance.

Fresh mint is also used to improve the taste of many blends and preparations.

Lemon balm tea has a wonderfully fresh taste and produces a relaxing, calming effect.

Sage (Salvia officinalis)

The leaves of the common sage plant, also known as garden sage, are used to make a slightly bitter-tasting herbal infusion that has antiseptic and anti-inflammatory properties, lowers the cholesterol level and stimulates the circulation and immune system.

Stinging nettle (Urtica)

This mild-tasting drink is made mainly from the dried leaves of the stinging nettle. It is a diuretic and protects against anaemia due to its high iron content.

In antiquity, sage tea was regarded as a magic cure and love potion.

Thyme (Thymus serpyllum)

An aromatic tea with antispasmodic and mucus-dissipating properties is made from the dried leaves of this strong-smelling medicinal and culinary herb.

Valerian (Valeriana officinalis)

This slightly bitter-tasting infusion is made from the dried root of the plant. It improves sleep and calms the nerves.

Tips for preparation

Most fruit, herbal, and spice teas are made by pouring boiling water on to the leaves (on average one teaspoonful per cup), leaving to steep for five to ten minutes, and then straining. In the case of blends, it is important to take note of all the different ingredients.

While infusions drunk purely for enjoyment can be lightly sweetened with honey, no sugar or artificial sweeteners should be used with medicinal teas.

Collecting herbs

Those wishing to pick their own wild herbs for use in wonderful-tasting and curative infusions should bear in mind the importance of behaving responsibly toward nature and should take care not to pick any protected species. Attention should also be paid to the correct harvesting times so that the different plants are picked when they are at their most effective. Plants should not be picked near freeways and other busy roads or in areas that have been heavily fertilized or that are affected by environmental pollutants.

Tea plantation in
Shizouka, Japan.
The first harvest
involves painstaking
manual labor.

Ingredients and Active Substances

Moreover, smaller younger leaves contain more caffeine than older larger leaves and stems.

Tea as a stimulant

In most people's minds, the pleasure of drinking tea is associated with an agreeable warmth and a certain cosy intimacy. Not only does tea stimulate the body and mind, it is also a perfect way of raising one's spirits.

It is caffeine that we have to thank for tea's stimulating properties. It was once known as teaine when it occurred in tea, but the single term "caffeine" is now used as the substances and compounds in tea and coffee are chemically identical.

However, the effects of the caffeine in a cup of tea are felt more slowly than those produced by the caffeine in coffee. This is because the caffeine in tea is bonded to the tannins and is only released gradually. The stimulant effects, on the other hand, last for a very long time.

William Ewart Gladstone described the effects of tea as follows:

"If you are cold, tea will warm you.
If you are too heated, it will cool you.
If you are depressed, it will cheer you.
If you are excited, it will calm you."

Green tea, a natural remedy and a mild stimulant, has a positive effect on both mind and body.

The composition, properties, and taste of a tea vary according to quality, which is influenced by a range of factors. Tannin and caffeine content, for example, differ from growing region to growing region and are also affected by climate, and the time and manner of picking.

Tea as a medicine

Traditional Chinese medicine takes a holistic approach. Not only does it regard body, mind, and soul as a unit, but also it sees mankind, nature, and the cosmos as being a single interconnected and constantly interacting entity.

In Chinese philosophy there are two aspects to all things: yin and yang. Yin and yang represent opposing forces such as male and female, cold and warm. It is vital for these opposing forces, which operate throughout the whole of nature, to be in harmony. Yin cannot exist without yang and vice versa. They flow into and out of each other, and together constitute a harmonious whole. Food and drink also play an important part in maintaining and restoring the harmonious balance between yin and yang, which is essential in order for one's life energy to flow unimpeded. This explains why tea is drunk with meals in China.

Each plant and the particular type of tea obtained from it have their own special properties. In the case of fruit and herbal infusions these effects have already been described and so we will now turn our attention to the main medicinal properties of black and, even more important, green tea. The quality of the tea has a considerable bearing on these medicinal properties as well as on taste.

The best way to store tea is in small jars or boxes, which help it to preserve its quality and individual taste.

Thanks to ingredients such as essential oils, minerals, and trace elements, green and black teas are natural medicine chests. The tannins in tea have anti-inflammatory properties, calm the stomach and intestines, and alleviate colds and respiratory tract problems. Infusion time plays a not inconsiderable role in this. The longer the tea brews, the more tannins are released into the liquid, giving it a slightly bitter taste. As green tea contains a higher level of tannins than black tea, it should not be left to brew for more than two minutes.

The latest research has shown that regular consumption of tea can reduce the risk of heart attacks and cancer.

Theophylline, which stimulates the circulation and relaxes the muscles, is present in small quantities in tea.

Tea is also rich in fluoride, a chemical element that strengthens the teeth and improves the ability of tooth enamel to withstand acids and bacteria, thereby inhibiting caries.

Green tea contains significant amounts of vitamin C, which is destroyed during the fermenting process.

Tea should never be brewed for longer than recommended, otherwise it can become bitter.

Last but not least, unsweetened green or black tea contains no calories and is therefore an ideal drink for anyone on a diet.

Tea as a household remedy

Used tea bags that have been left to cool are good for tired eyes.

Compresses soaked in cold tea can relieve mild sunburn.

Fish smells can be removed from pans by rubbing wet tea leaves into them.

Keen gardeners often fertilize their plants with brewed tea.

Japanese scientists have discovered that the tannins in tea absorb formaldehyde vapors. Anyone who cannot tolerate the smell of fresh paint or glue should therefore hang green or black teabags in the relevant rooms in order to reduce the concentration of formaldehyde in the atmosphere.

The right way to store tea

Green and black tea alike should be stored in cool, dry, and dark conditions, ideally in tight-closing containers made of pottery, glass, plastic, or porcelain. Opinion is divided on the virtues of metal. While many tea lovers advise against the storage of tea in metal containers, others are in favor of this choice of material as it offers a dark and airtight means of storage.

Under no circumstances should tea be stored near coffee or strong-smelling spices as this could impair the delicate aroma of the sensitive tea leaves. Equally damaging is steam from a stove or sink.

Tea caddies come in all shapes, sizes, and designs. Regardless of whether they are made of wood or metal, the most important thing is that the lids fit tightly.

The Refined Art of Making Tea

The tea ritual in China

The great tea master Lu Yu was the first person to recognize that in order for tea to be enjoyed to the full, a proper tea culture was needed. In his treatise on the preparation of tea he describes how the water is heated until it begins to form bubbles resembling fish eyes and until the boiling water starts to make the air sing. These are the signs that the water has reached the first stage. A pinch of salt is added and a few bamboo sticks dropped in to calm it down, then some of the water is removed. Next, powdered tea is added until it covers the surface of the water in a thin layer. The water previously removed is then added back in order to lower the temperature. As a general rule, tea was drunk hot from simple clay bowls that often curved outwards towards the top. This way of preparing tea gradually spread along the Silk Road.

Powdered tea is still common in remote mountain communities in central China and eastern Turkestan.

Many countries still observe tea rituals that developed over the course of several centuries.

The choices of tea, infusion method, tea service, and additives play important roles in the different tea ceremonies.

A similar though slightly different tea culture is shared by a number of nomadic peoples in Mongolia and Tibet who make a form of "tea soup."

The manner in which tea was enjoyed was refined considerably during the Song Dynasty (960–1279), although black tea bowls continued to be used in preference to all others because of the wonderful color contrast with the jade-green tea.

A little tea powder would be placed in a pre-warmed bowl and a small amount of hot water added, just enough to form a paste when stirred with a bamboo whisk. More water, now cooler, was then poured into the bowl and the liquid whisked until a layer of froth formed on the surface. During this process it was essential not to splash the water or moisten the edge of the bowl. At the imperial court the preparation of tea often took the form of a competition, the winning "tea master" being the one whose froth survived the longest.

By the end of the Song Dynasty, tea had become a trading commodity. Thanks to the activities of merchants, officials, and mandarins, ordinary people started to have access to a beverage that had once been the preserve of the imperial court. Imaginative merchants enhanced inferior grades of tea by adding fragrant essences and flowers—thus, the first scented teas came into being. These included jasmine, rose, and kwai flower.

The classic method of tea preparation

The development of the classic method of tea preparation still in use today (also known as the "two-pot method") began during the Ming Dynasty (1368–1644).

Yixing is famous for its exquisite ceramics, which are often used in the traditional tea ceremony.

The tea was no longer ground to a powder and compressed; instead whole leaves were used. Rapid developments in the manufacture of ceramics and porcelain resulted in new receptacles that enabled tea to be transported securely and also allowed the tea masters and others to store their teas for longer periods of time.

This Ming-era ceremony requires a cup for each tea drinker, two teapots (one of pottery, one of porcelain), and a water basin to catch the drips when, at a certain stage, hot water is poured over the teapots and cups. Once it has been warmed with hot water, the tea leaves are placed inside the pottery teapot and hot water (at about 176°F/80°C) added. This water is then immediately poured off. Hot water is added to the leaves again, the liquid left to steep for a period of one to two minutes, and the tea poured into the empty porcelain teapot.

China's most popular crockery during the Ming era was blue and white ware, known in China as Ching-Te-Chen porcelain after the place of its manufacture in Jiangxi province. Chinese porcelain became a highly desirable commodity and, for a long time, was considered a luxury in Europe.

Gong Fu Cha

The Chinese tea ceremony known as Gong Fu Cha also developed during the Ming Dynasty and has not changed substantially during the intervening period.

The ceremony originated in the southern Chinese province of Fujian. It is a tea-drinking ritual designed to regenerate the body and calm the mind while also celebrating the beauty of handmade utensils. Gong Fu Cha requires a number of teapots, a tea table that is either ceramic-topped, or made of bamboo or rosewood, and a dish to catch any excess water. Also essential for the proper enjoyment of the tea is a set of appropriate tea tools.

During the Gong Fu Cha ceremony the host sits at the tea table while the guests group around it. The teapot is filled with hot water, the lid replaced, and hot water poured over it from the outside. Next the tea bowls are warmed with water from the teapot. This procedure forms part of the preparation.

The actual making of the tea then begins. The teapot is filled up to a third full with tea leaves, and water poured on in a circular motion. The lid is replaced and water is again poured over the outside of the teapot.

This first infusion, which is immediately poured off into the individual bowls (to scent them), serves to "wash the tea." This process also opens the leaf pores and helps to reduce the bitterness of later infusions.

The pot is then filled with water a second time. The tea is poured after being left to steep for 10 to 30 seconds. The bowls are not filled one after the other, but a little at a time in order to ensure that everyone's tea is of equal strength. This ceremony continues in the same manner with each infusion being allowed 10 seconds more than its predecessor.

Tea ceremony etiquette

Older individuals are served first and the others wait patiently until they have begun to drink.

Only when all bowls have been filled do guests begin to drink.

The drinking vessel is always held between thumb and index finger and supported underneath by the middle finger.

The tea is tasted slowly. First its wonderful scent is enjoyed; then it is slurped noisily. This improves the taste of the tea by increasing the amount of oxygen taken in with it.

The pauses between infusions are used for chatting.

Tea tools and utensils

Scoop for extracting tea from the caddy.

Funnel for filling the teapot with tea.

Tongs for handling the lids, taking the tea bowls out of the water dish, or picking out and inspecting individual tea leaves.

Needle for clearing a spout blocked by tea leaves.

Tea bowls.

Pottery water dish for warming and rinsing teapot and bowls.

Hot water (ideally soft).

Cookies to help clear the palate between different varieties of tea.

The tea ritual in Japan

The Japanese tea ceremony grew out of rituals performed originally by Japanese monks. While previously an everyday act consisting of the preparation and drinking of tea, the tea ceremony (*chanoyu*) gradually mutated into the "way of tea" (*chado*), a path to self-awareness and a consciousness-training technique. *Do* translates as "way," meaning a spiritual way or path that lasts a lifetime. A number of different disciplines developed in Japan that all shared the same goal. These include Judo (the way of gentleness), Kendo (the way of the sword), Kyudo (the way of the bow), Kodo (the way of fragrance), and Kado (the way of flowers).

The way of tea as practiced today dates back to the renowned tea master Sen no Rikyu, who identified four essential principles: harmony (*wa*), respect (*kei*), purity (*sei*), and calm (*jaku*). Harmony relates to a oneness with nature, respect presupposes a reverence for all people and things, and purity involves not only external cleanliness but also purity of thought. If the first three principles, *wa*, *kei*, and *sei* are observed, it is believed that inner calm (*jaku*) will follow in time.

The way of tea is an ongoing learning process and a way of experiencing the harmony of the cosmos. Rikyu explained: "We evoke a feeling of coolness in summer, and warmth and security in winter. We burn charcoal and watch the water boil; we make tea and taste that it is good. There is no other secret." Yet it takes an enormous amount of practice to be able to conduct a tea ceremony.

In Japanese tea schools the art of *chado* and the tea ceremony is taught by specially trained tea masters. The rules of the tea ceremony vary to a certain degree depending on which school a tea master belongs to. Anyone who has an opportunity to experience a Japanese tea ceremony should seize it with both hands.

Originally part of the Japanese home, the tea room gradually developed into a separate tea house.

It is important for the host's physical gestures and state of mind to be in harmony with each other.

The host's gestures are economical and effective.

At the end of the meal, the host serves a sweet to accompany the thick tea (koicha) that follows.

A formal tea gathering (chaji)

A traditional tea gathering combined with a meal can last for hours. If the ceremony is held in a tea house with a "tea garden," a stroll through the garden is considered a special and integral form of inner preparation.

The tea ceremony is held using the prescribed tea utensils in a simple tea room whose floor is covered in rice mats.

The gestures of the tea master and the guests are both economical and effective, and follow prescribed procedures. The tea ceremony can last up to four hours or longer and is designed to free the guests from all their troubles and burdens.

There are two distinct tea ceremony seasons: the *furo* or summer season (May through October); and the *ro* or winter season (November through April). The word *furo* refers to a portable stove, while *ro* designates a hearth set into the floor. In terms of procedures, utensils, and general atmosphere, the two forms differ considerably from each other. The following description of a summer gathering is just one of a number of forms the ceremony can take.

The start

The guests gather in a waiting room at the specified time. Then they enter the garden together and sit on a bench to wait for the host to appear. The host greets them silently with a deep bow.

Next the guests stroll through the garden one after the other, and rinse their hands and mouth in a water basin.

The tea is whipped into a thick liquid with the bamboo whisk. The thick green tea, called koicha, *is the first of the two types of tea to be prepared.*

He serves a light meal in several courses, then ceremonially places more charcoal on the stove. He offers his guests something sweet in order to prepare their palates for the (unsweetened) tea to follow.

The guests leave the room and return to the garden to wait for the tea room to be made ready for the second part of the ceremony. When the room is fully prepared a gong is sounded and the guests return. They will now find a vase of flowers in the picture alcove in place of the scroll. Next to the stove and kettle there will be a fresh water container and in front of it a ceramic tea caddy (*chaire*) in a cloth cover. The host gradually brings in the other utensils such as the tea bowl and bamboo whisk (*chasen*), cleansing cloth, bamboo spoon, waste water bowl, bamboo ladle, and lid rest.

At this stage, the host begins to prepare the tea, employing firmly established holds and gestures. Using the bamboo ladle, he pours a little hot water into the tea bowl in order to cleanse it and the whisk. Then he empties the water into the waste water container.

The host spoons a generous amount of tea powder into the bowl, pours hot water on to it

The entrance to the tea room is small and low, which means that all the guests have to bow deeply and crawl rather than step into the room. This posture symbolizes both humbleness and respect, and eliminates all class differences. The clear message is that all people are equal.

The interior of the room is sparsely furnished. Tea master Rikyu believed that there should be nothing in the tea room to distract those present from the essential purpose. All the implements, decorations (even the scroll and flowers) and items of food are therefore chosen with the greatest of care and are precisely coordinated. But they are never purely aesthetic expressions and must not be allowed to distract the guests from their state of watchfulness and concentration, for the way of Zen is the focus of the tea ceremony.

In the picture alcove hangs a scroll depicting a Zen Buddhist thought or saying that relates to the occasion. This is examined in detail by each of the guests in turn. An iron kettle, in which water is quietly humming, sits on the stove. When all the guests are seated, the tea master or host appears and greets them individually.

Guests are offered a light sweet to enjoy with the second, thinner, tea (usucha).

Finally, a bowl of thin tea (called usucha) is prepared for each guest.

with the ladle and stirs the tea into a thick liquid with the bamboo whisk.

During this time the guests are as silent as possible and take in every noise made during the tea-making process: the humming of the kettle, the shuffling of feet on the *tatami* mats, the splashing of water as it is poured, the beating of the whisk and the rustling of the silk cloth.

Next, the host places the bowl containing the thick green tea (*koicha*) on the floor. The first guest picks it up, slowly drinks three mouthfuls of tea, wipes the edge of the bowl with a damp cloth and passes it to the next guest, who likewise takes three mouthfuls of tea. Afterwards, the host concludes this part of the tea ceremony by cleaning all the utensils and presenting them for the guests' inspection.

The host then adds more charcoal to the fire. The next part of the ceremony is far less formal and in contrast to the preparation of the *koicha*, during which barely a word is spoken, is accompanied by polite conversation. The host brings in a light sweet and the tea utensils with new tea bowls and a different variety of tea in a lacquerware tea caddy (*natsume*). This time he

prepares a bowl of frothy thin tea (*usucha*) for each of those present. After a brief farewell chat between the host and each of the guests in turn, the tea gathering comes to a close. The host sits alone in the empty tea room to reflect

silently for a few moments on the day's events. The best description of the Japanese tea ceremony is that of Dr. Sen Soshitsu, the 15th-generation Grand Master of the Urasenke School of Tea: "I hold a bowl of tea in my hands. In its green color I see all of nature. I close my eyes. Deep within me I see green mountains and the clear water of their springs. I sit alone or in a small circle of friends, fall silent and feel how all of this becomes a part of me."

The guest pays respect to the host and thanks him for the tea by bowing.

"Chatting, we enjoy a bowl of green tea –
Flowers shrouded in mist rise up and open
in the clouds."
Nishikoribe no Hikogimi

The tea ritual in Britain

Teatime is a national institution in Britain and afternoon tea in particular has enjoyed a long tradition. It is thought to go back to the 18th century when Anna, Duchess of Bedford, took to satisfying her late-afternoon pre-dinner hunger by taking tea with cakes and pastries.

Before long, afternoon tea started to be celebrated with some ceremony. The finest table linen and crockery would be brought out, and delicious sandwiches and cakes or petit fours served.

Later, tea began to be drunk in bed early in the morning, at breakfast and at high tea (which gradually developed into a main evening meal). A strong variety of tea is usually served in the afternoon. It is generally enjoyed with milk (the question of whether to put the

Teatime in Britain is a national institution that goes back to the 18th century.

milk in first or add it afterwards has never been satisfactorily resolved) and sweetened to taste.

The tea ritual in India

The Indians prepare their national drink with the same reverence they have toward their cuisine. Their tea is expected to be every bit as perfect as their favorite meal and as tasty as a pilau dish, and is served with sweet titbits.

As a rule, tea is enjoyed in India with a lot of milk. In many parts of the country spices such as cinnamon, cloves, aniseed, and cardamom are also added.

The tea ritual in Morocco

Although tea established itself in Morocco relatively late on, it is now a fixture at every mealtime. The job of preparing what is usually mint tea, a combination of green Gunpowder tea and fresh shoots of mint sweetened with sugar, generally falls to the man. During the ceremony, the tea is poured out of the bulbous teapot from a great height, filling the whole room with a wonderful aroma.

In many parts of India, tea is flavored with spices such as cardamom, cloves, aniseed or cinnamon. In Morocco, mint is a common flavoring.

On top of the water container sits a small pot containing super-strong tea (*zavarka*). A quarter of a glassful of tea concentrate is poured and the glass then filled up with hot water (*kipjatok*). The tea is served in glasses (normally with handles) rather than cups because this makes it easier to gauge the required strength of tea. The tea is usually enjoyed with a sugar cube or a spoonful of jam. Essential accessories include a teapot to hold the tea concentrate, a tray, and a drip bowl. Several types of tea are enjoyed in this manner, accompanied by sugar in crystal or candy form, milk and cakes, pastries, or cookies.

The tea ritual in Taiwan

The art of making tea in the traditional Chinese Gong Fu Cha manner is an integral part of daily life for people at all levels of Taiwanese society. The necessary equipment includes a tastefully and artistically decorated cedar or rosewood tea table. Equally tasteful and artistic is the ceramic ware, often from Yingko, whose potteries specialize in the manufacture from local raw materials of bowls, teapots, and kettles. The ceramics from this town are masterfully made using traditional techniques and are particularly valued by lovers of oolong tea.

During the tea ceremony in Taiwan, guests are handed a tea bowl and an aroma cup on a small rosewood tray. This is so that the tea lover can enjoy the fragrance of the tea before the tea master or mistress celebrates the tea ritual proper.

The tea ritual in Tibet

For centuries very little has changed in the way Tibetan butter tea is made. The son of Tibetan king Srong-Tsen-Gam-Po (629–698) introduced brick tea into the country in the 7th century. Due to the ease of transportation and the fact that it kept for longer, brick tea became widespread in central Asia and Russia. The

In Russia, tea is traditionally made using a samovar and drunk out of beautifully decorated tea glasses.

The tea ritual in Russia

In Russia a copper or brass receptacle known as a *samovar* (meaning self-brewer) traditionally occupies center stage in the tea-making process. Invented in the Caucasus around 250 years ago, samovars used to be heated by charcoal or a similar fuel and provided a steady supply of hot water all day long. Nowadays electric samovars are also common. Inside the base of the samovar is a metal cylinder that holds the charcoal. Hot water is extracted by means of a tap on the end of an outlet pipe.

In East Friesland, teatime takes place between two and three o'clock in the afternoon, and would not be complete without rock candy and cream.

The tea ritual in East Friesland

The East Frisians are thought of in Germany as the country's most "English" of tea drinkers. Even today every meal in the region is accompanied by a cup of tea. Teatime proper is traditionally between two and three o'clock in the afternoon, when the beverage is accompanied by cakes and pastries.

The actual pouring of the tea resembles a kind of ceremony. First of all, a large lump of rock candy (*Kluntje*) is placed into each of the cups (traditionally a shallow bowl shape with a handle), and the hot tea poured over it. The cup is not filled right to the top but just high enough for the sugar to be generously covered. The rock candy crackles softly, jumps around, and is said to be laughing. Next, a little unwhipped cream (*Rohm*) is carefully floated on to the surface of the tea using a specially curved spoon. The cream gradually sinks and then rises back up to the surface in little clouds (*Wulkje*). On no account should the tea be stirred. The enjoyment lies in first tasting the tea with the little clouds of cream in it, then the sharper taste of the tea underneath and finally the sweetened tea at the bottom of the cup.

traditional method of making it was to crush dried tea with a pestle and mortar, mix it with rice water, and press it into bricks weighing up to 6.5 pounds (3 kilograms).

Tea, of which the Tibetans still drink between 30 and 40 cups a day, has been the national drink of this mountain people ever since. Remnants of tea are stirred into a paste with ground barley, boiled up with fragments of tea brick, soda, and water, then salted and spiced. Later this tea concentrate is churned in a pipe with hot water and rancid-smelling yak's butter. The result is a thick beverage the color of cocoa. Unleavened bread made of corn, barley, or buckwheat is often eaten with it.

The tea ritual in South America

Mate tea is a national drink of sorts in many Latin American countries and is still often drunk out of the traditional vessel, a gourd called the *cuia*.

To prepare the tea, the *cuia* is first half filled with mate leaves, then topped up with cold or lukewarm water. Boiling water is never used for the first infusion.

After a short interval, a drinking pipe or straw known as the *bombilla* is pushed to the bottom of the gourd with the thumb, and the first, bitter infusion sucked up and spat out. The *cuia* is then filled with hot water and the mate is ready for drinking. Traditionally, the *cuia* is

passed between the guests. The drink must not be stirred with the *bombilla*, as the drinking pipe will become blocked. The mate leaves can be infused with hot water a number of times.

The tradition of the tea house and tea shop

China's first tea houses came into being during the Song Dynasty and developed under the Ming Dynasty into popular meeting places. During the Cultural Revolution, when large numbers of intellectuals and tea masters fled to Taiwan, these tea houses almost disappeared completely. However, a few (for example, in the provinces of Sichuan and Yunnan) managed to survive. More recently, old tea houses have been renovated as tourist attractions in parks and gardens all over the country and new ones built. They are also springing up in the suburbs and in smaller towns, although by and large they differ greatly to the way they once were. They are no longer sparsely decorated but generally very attractively fitted out. What's more, in addition to tea they often serve a wide range of nibbles and also light meals.

Not only is tea-drinking a favorite pastime among the older generation but also the tea house has become a popular venue for conducting business negotiations while also serving as a meeting place for young people keen to chat about sport, music, and anything else that interests them. On weekends the tea house is a popular venue for the whole family.

A traditional cuia *in which mate is made and from which it is drunk through a* bombilla.

The Japanese tea house

Originally the tea room was part of the Japanese home, a segregated area of the reception room. In addition to the opulent tea contests of the 14th century, social teas were held in formal reception rooms. Here too an emphasis was placed on pomp and splendor, and the rooms in which tea was served were often highly ostentatious. Murata Shuko initiated a move away from these large events to a smaller, dedicated tea room, and reduced the size of the tea room to the area taken up by four and a half *tatami* mats (roughly 9'4" x 9'4"/2.86 x 2.86 meters), an ideal space for a tea room. The square shape derives from Taoism. Due to the fixed size of the *tatami* mats it was only possible to create a square space using either two or four and a half mats. The square was a symbol of the four points of the compass, the four seasons (corresponding to the four sides of the room) and the five main elements, water, fire, earth, wood, and metal (represented by the five mats used). Contemplation of one's inner world and a desire to focus on the simple and the essential was reflected in the choice of

A Japanese tea house. The focus here is on the internal, the simple, the essential.

materials and equipment. This was taken a step further by Takeno Joo, who created the three-mat tea room and showed a preference for simple, natural materials and objects. This resulted in the first ever free-standing tea house (*sukiya*) set in a tea garden (*roji*), which represented a border between the outer and inner worlds.

A reduction of the tea room to the bare essentials was finally achieved by the famous tea master Sen no Rikyu. He reduced the space to two mats and developed the low entrance that placed the host and all the guests on the same footing, eliminating all class distinctions. The idea behind this was that nothing should be allowed to ruin the harmony of the gathering. Simplicity was the governing principle behind the whole occasion and determined the choice of building materials as well as the sparse decoration and utensils.

Sen no Rikyu's successors, in particular his grandson Sen Sotan (1578–1658), renewed the entire culture of tea in the spirit of Rikyu's ideas.

The English tea house

At the beginning of the 18th century England's coffee houses were transformed into tea houses. As they were the exclusive preserve of men, women started to enjoy the new custom at home. In 1717 Thomas Twining opened the first tea room to welcome everyone. This was soon followed by other public tea rooms and gardens, where a refined tea culture was enjoyed, often accompanied by an orchestra.

The tradition of tea rooms and tea gardens still exists in England today, though generally without the musical entertainment or such high standards regarding the quality of the tea. Naturally the emphasis is still on the tradition of afternoon tea, which is no less an integral part of everyday life in Britain.

Indeed, British playwright Alan Ayckbourn suggests that the English teatime is the only immutable institution on earth.

A Chinese saying suggests that where noble people gather happily over tea, the roof of their home touches heaven.

Preparation Tips and Accessories

Because of the wealth of different varieties available, when choosing a tea we recommend that you seek advice from a specialist retailer. Here you will be able to ask about how much tea to use and how long to let it brew. The main factors that influence the infusion time are the type of tea and personal taste.

In any event, the tea should always be freshly prepared and drunk straight away. Whatever method is used for keeping tea warm, it always tastes best fresh.

Water

After the quality of the tea, the next most important factor affecting the final result is the water.

The Chinese tea masters had a preference for fresh spring water, ideally from a mountain spring. As this option is not normally available to us, we generally have to make do with tap water.

Partially demineralized water is ideal for making tea, but heavily chlorinated or fluorinated water should be avoided. Other unsuitable types of water include excessively hard water and water containing high levels of salt, iron, or oxidized magnesium.

These days water purifiers are readily available; these allow us quickly and easily to decalcify our tap water. All we have to do is regularly change the filter cartridge.

Chinese tea masters use only spring water when making tea.

From the choice of tea to the way it is prepared, every aspect has a bearing on the flavor of the final result. Each of us should therefore seek our own "way of tea." That said, we would like to offer a few basic tips to help you on your way.

The tea bag

The universally popular tea bag is thought to have been invented in 1904 when American tea importer Thomas Sullivan sent out a number of samples in small silk bags. His customers found them a highly practical way of making tea. As demand grew, muslin replaced silk before being substituted later by paper.

Much earlier, when the counterfeiting of tea—either by dyeing it or mixing in other plant-based substances—had become widespread, a Briton named John Horniman came up with a solution. He started to sell tea in sealed paper bags bearing his name as a guarantee of authenticity. However, this entrepreneurial gentleman sealed his bags with glue and the resulting tea tasted of either glue or paper.

Attempts were later made to manufacture cotton tea bags but these gave the tea a musty taste.

It eventually took an engineer from the Dresden-based company Teekanne to develop a tea-packing machine capable of making affordable tea bags without the use of any glue. Today the tea bag is regularly used for all kinds of tea and has become a familiar part of our lives. It is not so much the shape of the tea bag but its size that is important. There must be enough room for the tea to circulate properly inside.

While the general quality of tea bags has improved considerably over recent years, there are still significant differences between them. Tea drinkers wishing to get the best from them would be well advised to visit a specialist retailer.

The tea bag has been making tea drinkers' lives easier since 1904. However, real tea connoisseurs and enthusiasts refuse to use what they see as the "fast food alternative."

Green tea

Whichever individual sort you prefer, green tea should never be made with boiling water or it will acquire a bitter taste.

First of all, the teapot and bowls or cups should be warmed. After boiling, the water should be left to cool to between 140 and 194°F (60 and 90°C) depending on the quality of the tea. Once it has cooled to the right temperature, place one heaped teaspoonful of green tea per person into the teapot and pour in the water, ensuring that the tea leaves are able to float around freely. After a maximum of two minutes (according to taste), pour the tea into the bowls or cups. Green tea is normally drunk without anything in it. The tea leaves should not be left in the teapot or the tea will become bitter. Depending on quality, green tea can be infused up to three times, with each infusion taking slightly longer that the last.

Black tea

Black tea should always be made with fresh soft water, as hard water impairs the flavor. In general a few minutes of boiling will be enough to decalcify the water. Filtered water is, of course, highly recommended.

The best way to make black tea is with a separate brewing pot. First, place the required amount of tea in the pot. Then measure out and boil a sufficient volume of water. A timer should be set for the correct infusion time and the hot water then poured in. After the appropriate length of time, pour through a fine sieve into a serving pot. For the correct amount of tea and brewing time, follow the instructions on the tea packet.

Sugar, honey, milk, cream, or lemon can be added according to individual taste.

Green or black tea always tastes best freshly brewed.

Rich green tea bushes hug the slopes of India's Havukal tea gardens.

This tea plantation is also in India—at Singampatti.

Here, then, are a few tips and suggestions concerning accessories and additives.

Cotton tea net

"Tea socks," which are readily available in a range of different sizes, quickly take on the scent of the particular tea for which they are used. They also start to look rather unsightly with prolonged use. Those who like to use cotton tea nets in spite of these drawbacks should consider using a different one for each different variety of tea.

Paper tea filter

Paper tea filters should be as large as possible so that the tea leaves can expand inside and move around freely. However, a lot of tea drinkers find the taste of the filter paper unpleasant and off-putting.

Sieve insert

Teapot sieve inserts are available in stainless steel, plastic, pottery, and glass. The important thing is that they are big enough to allow the tea leaves to swim around freely. These days a lot of teapots are sold with a matching sieve insert.

Regardless of whether they are made of stainless steel, pottery, or glass, teapot sieve inserts should always allow the tea leaves enough room to swim around freely.

Tea accessories

Anyone wanting to make teatime a special occasion will attach particular importance to using the right crockery and accessories. Both the preparatory steps and the actual making of the tea can create a sense of anticipation and contribute to the pleasure to follow. It is important to leave enough time for this.

A table beautifully laid with your best china can be a source of great enjoyment. And no good host would ever allow him or herself to be deprived of the job of preparing and serving the tea. As far as the "ceremony" itself is concerned, it is perfectly acceptable to borrow elements from all the different tea cultures. One might wish to serve cakes or cookies with the tea or even, in the English tradition, a few sandwiches.

Small stove

A small stove can be a useful way of keeping the tea warm—but only when the pot is full. If there is only a little tea in the pot it will gradually become hotter and darker, and acquire a bitter taste when kept warm this way. A thermos teapot can be a good alternative— particularly when you have trouble finding time to make tea at home.

Tea egg

Tea eggs, a form of infuser made of metal or porcelain, are a common tea-making tool. However, as the tea leaves rapidly expand it can often be difficult for the water to flow in and out of the egg and wash around the leaves, which are unable to release their vital ingredients as a result. We would not, therefore, necessarily recommend tea eggs.

Tea machines

Electric tea machines provide a quick and easy way of making tea. They are sometimes preferred in offices but can be relatively difficult to clean.

Teapot

A teapot and tea service should never be used for other beverages such as coffee.

Real connoisseurs keep a separate teapot for each different variety of tea because a Darjeeling, for example, would be completely overpowered by the aroma of an Assam. A separate teapot is also needed for smoked or scented teas and similarly for fruit and herbal teas.

Teapots come in all shapes, sizes, and materials. If a teapot's sieve insert is too small, the best solution would be to brew the tea in a separate pot without using a sieve so that the tea leaves can swim around freely. As soon as the tea is ready, it can be transferred to another teapot set aside for serving.

Small stoves come in many different designs but beware: the constant heat can affect the taste of the tea.

Japan in particular has a long tradition of cast-iron teapots.

The epitome of Chinese tea culture: a teapot of the finest porcelain.

Unglazed pottery teapots soon acquire the desired "patina" inside.

Teapots made of glass

Glass teapots are extremely easy to clean and there is no possibility of them harboring alien and unpleasant aromas. This means one teapot will suffice for all the different varieties. Glass teapots are also attractive to look at and provide a hint of the pleasure to come.

Teapots made of cast iron

Because of the thickness of the material, tea stays warm for a very long time in cast-iron teapots, which are sometimes enameled inside. In Japan there is a long tradition of cast-iron teapots. There they are preferred without interior enameling, as rust is seen as an important source of iron for the human body.

Teapots made of porcelain

Porcelain teapots are usually glazed a light color inside and gradually take on an increasingly dark hue with frequent use.

Teapots made of silver

Silver teapots were once elaborately crafted and seen as a sign of wealth. However, they are only able to keep the tea warm for a short period of time.

Teapots made of pottery

Pottery teapots, usually glazed on the outside, soon acquire a thoroughly desirable "patina" inside. Pottery teapots should not be cleaned with washing-up liquid or scrubbed but simply rinsed with clean water and left to dry in the air. In the case of new teapots, make a potful of strong tea (using leaves) and leave to soak into the pot for a whole day in order to help the patina get started.

Teacups

Suitable drinking vessels include the finest delicate porcelain cups and saucers, glasses, and robust ceramic bowls.
While small bowls without handles are used in China and Japan, small tea glasses are favored in Russia and Morocco. Tea bowls should be wide-brimmed to allow the aroma to unfold properly.
The now common teacup with handle was a British invention inspired by the mugs in which hot toddies used to be served. In certain

situations—in the office, for example—a large stable mug is not a bad idea.

The most sensible course of action is to choose the right cup for the right occasion and mood rather than using the same one all the time. When you have guests it is nice to be able to use a complete tea service that includes a sugar bowl, milk jug, and cake plate.

Lidded cup

The lidded cup, which is common in China, is the only vessel needed to make a good cup of tea. The requisite volume of tea leaves is placed directly in the cup and hot water added. Once the tea has been left to infuse for a sufficient length of time, the lid is pushed back just far enough for the tea to be drunk from the cup, ensuring that the leaves stay behind in the cup. The lid of what is usually a porcelain cup ensures that the temperature inside the cup does not drop too quickly, and that the leaves do not escape and also protect the beverage from annoying insects. Cups of this kind are a good alternative to the teapot.

Kettle

It makes no real difference whether the water is boiled in a stainless steel kettle on the hob or in an electric kettle. Those who live in hard water areas are advised to use a stainless steel kettle as they are more efficient at collecting and holding back the limescale.

Tea timer

Hourglasses and digital timers help to ensure that the tea brews for exactly the right length of time. All too often we make a pot of tea, then decide to use the brewing time to do something else—and forget about the tea altogether! Timers that emit a noise when the desired length of time has elapsed are particularly useful.

Yixing, in China, is famous for its ceramic ware.

Tea cosies

Normally made of wool or quilted fabric, teapot covers help the tea to stay warm for longer. Unless absolutely necessary, it is better to do without them and brew a fresh pot of tea instead.

Tea infuser

Tea infusers come in a range of different sizes. They consist of two hinged wire mesh cups attached to a handle with an opening/closing mechanism. They should always be large enough for the water to wash freely around the leaves.

A tea infuser should always be large enough to allow the hot water to wash around the leaves.

Tea additives

Real connoisseurs drink their tea—particularly green tea—unsweetened in order to enjoy the full aroma and health-promoting effects. It seems probable that sugar, honey, milk, and lemon were originally added to cover up the taste of inferior-quality teas. The custom of drinking black tea with milk and sugar developed out of the English tradition. The Dutch, who were the first to import tea into Europe, added milk to strong black tea in order to tone down its bitterness.

There is another, historical explanation for the addition of milk. The first tea ship to reach Europe also had Chinese porcelain in its hold. Europeans feared that hot tea could damage the thin-walled cups, and therefore poured a little cold milk in first in order to protect them and cool down the tea.

The important thing with additives is to get the amount right. But that is a question of personal preference.

Alcohol

A good tea does not require the addition of any alcohol, but for many tea drinkers a shot of rum or (as in Scotland) a wee glass of whiskey adds to the pleasure.

Honey

When sweetening tea with honey it is important to use neutral rather than flavored varieties.

Milk and cream

Milk or cream should be poured into the cup first. The very hot water will prevent any little clots of fat from forming which would impair the taste of the tea.

Less suitable are condensed milk or coffee cream. But here, too, there are some dyed-in-the-wool tea drinkers who prefer their tea with condensed milk.

Sweeteners

Sweeteners, such as those used by diabetics and the figure-conscious, are kind on the metabolism, and are generally calorie-free.

Lemon

A little lemon juice helps to make more astringent, powerful varieties of tea easier to drink and ensures that there is no bitter aftertaste. If whole slices of lemon are used, it is important to use untreated, or unwaxed, lemons. The custom of adding lemon slices to tea originated in Russia as a way of covering up the taste of dust acquired by the tea during transportation.

Sugar

White rock candy: these large sugar crystals are made from concentrated sugar solutions. Many of those who sweeten their tea like to use white rock candy. Others use it so that their preferred light tea varieties do not become discolored.

Brown rock candy: this is made by heating and caramelizing highly concentrated sugar solution, then leaving it to form crystals.

Raw cane sugar: this partly refined light-brown sugar cane gives the tea a slightly darker hue and dissolves quickly.

Refined sugar: this is ordinary white household sugar obtained from an extremely pure sugar solution and comes in a range of grain sizes.

Rock candy is often used instead of sugar as a tea sweetener.

Glossary

Assam
Located in India, the largest continuous growing region in the world.

Attractive
Uniform leaf in terms of shape and color.

Blend
A mixture of more than one variety of tea.

Body
Fullness of strength and aroma.

Bold
Coarse leaf that does not match its grade.

Brick tea
Brick tea, once common in Russia, Tibet, and central Asia due to the ease with which it could be transported, was made by compressing leaves and dust into blocks.

Bright
Refers to color.

Broken = B
A grade of tea consisting of leaves made smaller by rolling or cutting.

Broken Orange Pekoe = BOP
A high-quality grade of tea consisting of leaves that have been broken and reduced in size.

Broken Pekoe = BP
A medium-quality grade of tea consisting of leaves that have been broken and reduced in size.

Brownish
Brown coloration of dry leaf resulting from excessively high drying temperature.

Caffeine
The caffeine in tea, previously known as teaine, is released more slowly than the caffeine in coffee and its effects last for a correspondingly longer length of time.

Ceylon
The former British colony, now called Sri Lanka, is the world's third largest tea-growing region.

Choppy
A hacked-up leaf.

Clean
When used to describe the dry leaf it means the tea contains no stems, dust, or impurities. With reference to the beverage it means no unpleasant aftertaste.

Coarse
Having an unpleasant aftertaste.

Cold-weather tea
Tea from Assam (south-west India) and Sri Lanka that is picked between January and March.

Contamination
Having impaired color and taste.

Crepy
Refers to crimped leaves.

CTC
Stands for "crushing, tearing and curling," a mechanized procedure that reduces the necessary fermentation time.

Darjeeling
Tea-growing region surrounding the town of Darjeeling in north-east India. This is where the world's most prized teas are grown.

Dark
Refers to the color of tea leaves after infusion.

Dry
Refers to the taste.

Drying
The fourth stage in the production of black tea, involving the drying of the leaves in hot air following fermentation.

Dust
Finely crushed and sieved tea leaves used in the production of tea bags.

Earl Grey
A variety of black tea flavored with natural oil of bergamot, a citrus fruit.

Earthy
Fresh, earthy aroma and taste.

English blend
A British blend consisting ideally of Ceylon, Darjeeling, and Assam teas.

Even
Regularity of leaf in terms of color and shape.

Fannings
Small leaf particles obtained as a result of sieving that are larger than Dust and smaller than Broken. Used mainly for tea bags.

Fermentation
Oxidation process that plays an important part in the manufacturing of black tea. During this process the tannin content is reduced, the green leaves turn red-brown, and the aromatic substances are able to unfold fully.

First flush
The first tea harvest after a gap in picking.

Flowery
Used to describe the tender young leaf.

Flowery Orange Pekoe = FOP
A high-quality grade of tea made from leaf tips that are not yet fully developed.

Flush
New shoot on a tea bush.

Fruity
Unpleasant taste caused by a bacterial infection.

Golden Flowery Orange Pekoe = GFOP
A Darjeeling Leaf tea made with tips and young leaves.

Green
Undesirable hue after infusion caused by excessively short processing.

Green tea
Tea that has been dried but not fermented. The green color of the leaves is preserved.

Gritty
Leaves that are excessively hard and dry.

Gunpowder
The leaves of this famous green tea are rolled into tight pellets, hence its name.

Hard
Pungent, bitter taste.

High-grown
Highland tea characterized by a delicate, flowery taste.

Indonesian tea
Tea grown predominantly in Sumatra and Java, used mainly for blending.

Irregular
Uneven leaf size.

Kenya
Africa's main tea-growing country.

Kluntje
Regional name for the large pieces of rock candy used to sweeten tea in East Friesland.

Leaf
A high-quality grade of tea consisting of whole and almost unbroken leaves.

Malty
A desirable taste reminiscent of malted grains.

Milled
Leaf that has passed through a cutter or miller.

Mixed
Refers to the uneven coloration of the leaf or the variety of teas in a blend.

Moldy
A stale or musty, undesirable taste.

Monsoon tea
Tea of average quality harvested during the monsoon season in northern India.

Nilgiri
Tea-growing region in southern India with tea gardens at over 6,560 feet (2,000 meters) above sea level.

Oolong
This semi-fermented tea sometimes referred to as "yellow tea" is produced mostly in Taiwan and China.

Orange Pekoe = OP
Leaf tea made from the finest, uppermost parts of the young shoot.

Pekoe = P
Pekoe refers to the third leaf below the tip of the shoot.

Pekoe Souchong
The fourth to sixth leaves below the leaf bud.

Pu-erh tea
A green tea from China that is bacterially fermented for years and is also sold under the name "red tea."

Red tea
Also known as pu-erh tea.

Rock candy
Large crystals of sugar used to sweeten tea (mainly the white variety).

Samovar
Meaning "self-brewer," this piece of equipment is common above all in Russia.

Scorched
Impaired taste or color as a result of over-firing.

Second flush
Tea with a powerful, spicy aroma picked in May and June.

Smoky

Smoky taste caused by a non-airtight drying device.

Souchong

Name used to describe particular varieties of tea with broad, open leaves.

Tannin

In green and black tea, tannins bond the caffeine and release it slowly. They also have a calming effect on the mucous membranes of the stomach and gut.

Tea ceremony

The Japanese tea ceremony developed out of Zen Buddhism and follows a strict, prescribed form.

Tea rose

The tenderest leaves from the first picking are assembled into decorative floral arrangements that attain their full beauty when infused in hot water.

Tea school

Japanese establishments in which the art of the tea ceremony is taught by specially trained tea masters.

Theophylline

Both black and green tea contain small amounts of this substance that dilates the blood vessels and bronchial tubes.

Thin, weak

An infusion lacking body.

Tip

The end of the leaf bud, which is covered in fine hairs.

Tippy Golden Flowery Orange Pekoe = TGFOP

A top-quality Darjeeling tea containing a high proportion of tips.

Well-twisted

Refers to the dry leaf.

White tea

A precious unfermented tea made in China from young leaf buds covered in downy white hairs.

Withering

The first stage in the production of tea whose purpose is to reduce the water content of the leaves.

Publication details

This is a Parragon Publishing Book

Copyright © 2007 Parragon Books Ltd
Queen Street House
4 Queen Street
Bath BA1, 1HE, UK

Layout: Ute Gierstorfer/Natalie Blei, alex media, Gierstorfer, Ferstl & Reichert GbR, Augsburg
Produced by: Natalie Blei/Petra Hammerschmidt, alex media, Gierstorfer, Ferstl & Reichert GbR, Augsburg
Concept: Ursula Mohr/Michaela Mohr
Editing: Michaela Mohr/Michael Kraft, mimo-booxx/textwerk., Augsburg; Konstanze Allnach, Augsburg

US edition produced by: Cambridge Publishing Management Ltd
Translation: Richard Elliott
Editing: Sandra Stafford
Proofreading: Juliet Mozley

Important note: All information and data in this book have been carefully researched and checked to the best of our knowledge. However, the author, the publisher and its representatives cannot be held liable for errors or omissions in this book and for any loss, damage or expense (whether direct or indirect) suffered by a third party relying on any information contained in this book.

ISBN: 978-1-4054-8967-6

Printed in Malaysia

Picture credits

© Dave Bartruff/CORBIS 63 left, 64, 89; © Bettmann/CORBIS 19; © Bennett Dean; Eye Ubiquitous/CORBIS 23; © Free Agents Limited/CORBIS 39; © Historical Picture Archive/CORBIS 18; © Julie Houck/CORBIS 81; © Karen Kasmauski/Corbis 57; © Johansen Krause/Archivo Iconografico, SA/CORBIS 16 top; © Chris Lisle/CORBIS 27; © Frank Lukasseck/ zefa/CORBIS 43; Kai Mewes, Munich 4, 8, 10, 11, 12, 13, 14, 15, 16 bottom, 24, 28, 40, 41, 42, 44, 45, 46, 47, 48, 49, 50, 51, 52, 53, 54, 55, 56, 58, 59, 60, 61, 62, 63 right, 66, 67, 68, 69, 70, 71, 72, 73, 74, 75, 76, 77, 78, 79, 80, 82, 83, 84, 86, 87, 88, 90, 91, 93, 94, 95; © Richard Powers/CORBIS 34; © Stapleton Collection/CORBIS 21 top; TeeGschwendner GmbH, Meckenheim 5, 7, 9, 20, 21 bottom, 22, 25, 26, 29, 30, 31, 32, 33, 35, 36, 37, 38, 85; © Underwood & Underwood/ CORBIS 17.

Acknowledgments

Special thanks to the "KanShoAn" tea house at the Urasenke School in Munich for the tea ceremony and friendly advice,
Kai Mewes, Munich, for his commitment to the project and outstanding photography,
Alexander Dirrichs, TeeGschwendner, Munich, for the provision of materials and expert technical advice,
and TeeGschwendner GmbH, Meckenheim for their friendly support and the provision of photographic material.